"True service is close to the heart of all who are following hard after Jesus. For this reason I welcome *Full Service* by Siang-Yang Tan. Dr. Tan has wonderfully distilled and critiqued the vast literature on servanthood and leadership, and in addition, given us practical insights into how servanthood looks in daily life. *Full Service* is itself a genuine act of service."

Richard J. Foster, founder, RENOVARÉ

"Siang-Yang Tan is a prolific reader and thinker. In *Full Service* he distills the essence of an *enormous* amount of Christian thought on what mattered most to Jesus. I have benefited as a student, beginning writer, and friend from Siang-Yang's servanthood. This book is an act of servanthood for you!"

John Ortberg, author, *God Is Closer Than You Think;*
teaching pastor, Menlo Park Presbyterian Church

"Finally, the cart has been put back behind the horse! With his typical style that is scholarly, biblically based, and accessible, Siang-Yang Tan reminds us that Jesus' call to servanthood is both primary and universal. Leadership is a secondary calling that is given to a few. Because the phrase 'servant-leader' may have the same ego appeal as 'tither-tycoon' to our fast-growth-oriented culture, it is timely to receive this gentle reminder from Dr. Tan that the secret of true servanthood is developing a friendship with Jesus."

Gary W. Moon, editor, *Conversations* journal;
author, *Falling for God*

"This superb book on servanthood reflects the exceptional wisdom and the spiritual depth for which Dr. Tan has become known through his many years of preaching, counseling, and writing. If you want to know what it means to be truly a servant of Christ—the highest of all callings—this is the book for you. I recommend it enthusiastically!"

Donald A. Hagner, George Eldon Ladd
Professor of New Testament, Fuller Theological Seminary

"The message of this book is biblical, balanced, and counter-cultural. But more so, it touches me deeply because of my personal relationship with Siang-Yang—he lives out what he writes in his personal life and ministry."

Chi-Hok Wong, president,
First Evangelical Church Association

FULL SERVICE

Moving *from* Self-Serve Christianity *to* Total Servanthood

SIANG-YANG TAN

Grand Rapids, Michigan

Published by Baker Books
a division of Baker Publishing Group
P.O. Box 6287, Grand Rapids, MI 49516-6287
www.bakerbooks.com

Second printing, August 2006

Printed in the United States of America

Library of Congress Cataloging-in-Publication Data

Tan, Siang-Yang, 1954–
Full service : moving from self-serve Christianity to total servanthood / Siang-Yang Tan.
p. cm.
Includes bibliographical references.
ISBN 10: 0-8010-6564-X (pbk.)
ISBN 978-0-8010-6564-4 (pbk.)
1. Christian life. I. Title.
BV4501.3.T36 2006
248.4—dc22 2005032256

To my mother, Madam Chiow Yang Quek,
whose life has been an exemplary model of servanthood,
with love, gratitude, and prayers

Contents

Foreword by Larry Crabb 9
Acknowledgments 13
Preface 15

1. Jesus' Call to Servanthood 19
2. Learning from the Master Servant—Jesus 25
3. Serving Our Best Friend 30
4. Servanthood Versus Servitude 40
5. Servanthood Versus Servant Leadership 47
6. True Service Versus Self-Righteous Service 64
7. Servanthood and Suffering 74
8. Servanthood and Humility 88
9. Servanthood and Rest 105
10. Servant Evangelism and Warfare 116
11. Servanthood in the Church 134
12. Servanthood in the Home 151
13. Servanthood in the Workplace and School 167
14. Living for Eternity 179

Notes 191

Foreword

I remember sitting in lavish gardens near Capetown, South Africa, sipping tea with Dr. David Broughton Knox. Our wives were exploring the stunning display of God's love of beauty all around us as we were enjoying rich conversation in its midst. Dr. Knox, for years principal of Moore Theological College in Sydney, Australia, was regarded by many who knew him as the finest theological mind of his day.

Aware of both the beauty surrounding me in the gardens and the brilliance sitting across from me at the table, a troubling question came to mind. "Dr. Knox," I asked, "why do people have so many problems? With all the potential for beauty, why is there so much ugliness and sorrow in our lives?"

With a mind that had long since left platitudes behind and for decades had traveled through the depths of disturbing reality guided only by biblical revelation, Dr. Knox replied in about three seconds, "Oh, it all boils down to self-centeredness, doesn't it." It was a statement, not a question, delivered humbly but with the authority of a man living on the far side of complexity.

That conversation took place two decades ago when I was still in my early forties. Those few words from Dr. Knox confirmed a suspicion that had been worming its way into my mind since graduate school days, the suspicion that beneath our struggles and joyless existence lies an often unrecognized, deeply loved, and mostly uncriticized passion to serve ourselves. And in Christians, that passion reveals itself most often in the assumption that God exists to cooperate with our self-centered agenda.

Siang-Yang Tan appropriately labels that distortion *self-serve Christianity*. Call it what you will—primary narcissism, old-fashioned self-centeredness, pride, character weakness—the problem is real. And it has more power to soil beauty and to mess up our personal lives and relationships than any other problem.

True servanthood, the opposite of self-serve Christianity, grows out of a human spirit filled with God's Spirit. Self-centeredness, on the other hand, is the fruit of the flesh, that horrible energy in every human soul that is unchangeably anti-God, that lie-believing conviction that recognizes no greater good than one's own subjective sense of well-being, that passionate resolve to pursue one's own interests with no thought that serving God might, in the long run, actually serve one's best interests.

Self-serve Christianity, our pervasive perversion of the real thing, not only accommodates the flesh, it attempts to socialize it with external goodness and then to pass it off as spiritual maturity. Beneath so much of what looks like good Christian living is the stubborn attitude that thinks God really exists to serve us. His pleasure isn't the point. Ours is. And we think there's a more direct and immediate way to secure our well-being than to live for his glory. *Our* felt desires now fill the spotlight. *Our* needs have assumed greater priority than his pleasure.

As I look around the world, including the church, and look into people's hearts, including mine, I see no worse evil than self-obsession. It's the root of every other expression of evil.

And I see no greater battle in the *regenerate* human soul than the too often hidden conflict between self-obsession and God-obsession. It shows up in every relationship, every conversation, every sentence. And I believe that the only path to real victory in this fierce battle is to become true servants.

Which brings me to the book you are about to read. Psychologist Siang-Yang Tan clearly and with gentle wisdom lets us see what true servanthood looks like and illumines the narrow path that gets us there.

Without ever compromising his foundation in Scripture, Dr. Tan artfully draws from psychological research, personal stories, and respected thinkers to bow us low enough and lift us high enough to see the real beauty revealed only in becoming a servant to all. Among his many rich insights, he rightly challenges the familiar notion of servant leadership as sometimes allowing *leading* to eclipse *serving*.

As I read the book, I could see an underlying theme that moved my spirit. It's this: when we recognize the incomparable beauty of Christ, when we delight in how he served his Father (and us) to the point of death, when we're drawn to his revelation of the beauty found only in the relationships among the Trinity, then and only then will the call to total servanthood be irresistibly attractive.

The beauty of Christ fills every page of this rich invitation issued by Dr. Tan to become true servants of God and each other.

Let me add a personal word. Siang-Yang is the right person to write this book. I know of no follower of Jesus more devoted to serving his Lord and his Lord's people. He serves me by praying every day for me and my family.

When Rachael (my wife) and I received devastating news some years ago that shredded our hearts, God provided Siang-Yang to serve us. Those moments spent together in conversation with God as Siang-Yang brought us before the Father continue to provide a rich taste of what you'll read about in this book. Dr. Tan lives what he writes.

Let me ask you to put the book down for a few minutes before reading on. Pray. Pray the Lord's Prayer. Pray that God's Spirit will reach deep into your heart both to expose the self-serving energy that remains within you and to reveal the beauty of servanthood that your soul longs to know.

Pray that thousands, millions, will recognize the life-changing truths that self-service destroys beauty (it never lives up to its promise), and that serving others out of a soul obsessed with God, at *any* cost to oneself (shame, rejection, disappointment) restores a beauty beside which the gardens near Capetown pale in comparison.

And pray that God will use this book to hallow his name, to bring his kingdom to earth, to further the reach of his will into many lives, especially yours.

Larry Crabb, founder and director, NewWay Ministries, author of *Inside Out, Shattered Dreams, The Pressure's Off, SoulTalk*, and *The PAPA Prayer*

Acknowledgments

I would like to first thank Don Stephenson, director of publications at Baker Publishing Group, for his interest in and support of my writing of this book. I would also like to thank Mary Wenger and the staff at Baker for their helpful editorial feedback and revisions.

I deeply appreciate Larry Crabb for so kindly writing the foreword. I am especially grateful and indebted to many intercessors and prayer partners for their prayer support for me during the writing of this book. I want to make special mention of the Wednesday night prayer meeting group at my church, prayer partners of RENOVARÉ and the RENOVARÉ Board/Team, and the members of my small group. They are all true servants of Jesus Christ!

I also want to thank Fuller Theological Seminary and my church First Evangelical Church Glendale for graciously providing me with a sabbatical, during which I completed the writing of this book. The excellent administrative and word-processing help of Betsy Stewart and Rachel Hall at Fuller and Lynn Mori at my church is gratefully acknowledged. I also appreciate the word-processing support of Brad Knetsch and Anna Hutts with an earlier draft of this book.

My daughter Carolyn provided helpful editorial feedback on an earlier draft of the book, for which I am very grateful. I gladly acknowledge the love and support of Angela, my wife, and Carolyn and Andrew, our grown children, in my life and work, including my writing. I deeply love and appreciate each one of them.

I have chosen to lovingly dedicate this book to my mother, Madam Chiow Yang Quek, who is an amazing example of a humble servant.

Above all, I want to thank God for calling me, through his loving grace and mercy, to be a servant of Jesus Christ, my best friend.

Preface

Much has been written in recent years on leadership, including Christian leadership. Each year, key leadership conferences are well attended by pastors, church leaders, and others, myself included. Unfortunately, there has been a tendency to uncritically borrow models of management and leadership from the secular world and to apply them too quickly to the church and parachurch organizations. I have been deeply concerned for a number of years that the heavy emphasis on leadership and leadership development in contemporary Christian circles may be misplaced. Leadership and leadership development are important and have their rightful place in Christian ministry. However, from a biblical perspective, servanthood or following Jesus all the way in true discipleship is more foundational and central in Christian life and ministry. Such servanthood can also be described as "Living in Jesus all the way!"

It has been said that the church is the hope of the world, and leaders are the hope of the church. I have become convinced over the years that it is more correct, biblically speaking, to state that Christ through the church is the hope of the world and *servants* are the hope of the church.

God has called us *first* to servanthood, not leadership. Servanthood 101 is the foundational course of life and ministry for disciples or followers of Jesus Christ. Servanthood 101 should also be the foundational course of any leadership training program or curriculum for those who may be called by God to serve in leadership.

When we have the right kind of servant attitude—servanthood that comes from being centered in Christ and following him in loving humility and caring compassion for the people we serve—the Lord will keep us in his perfect peace as we steadfastly focus our minds and hearts on him and trust in him alone (Isa. 26:3). We will not be easily affected by the people who are cynical and critical of us. We will not be quickly upset by the people we serve for not appreciating or noticing us. We serve the Lord as our audience of one. We do not serve in order to receive the praises and affirmations of people who can be fickle in both their praise and their criticism. Being human, we enjoy and appreciate the support and encouragement of others. However, in true servanthood, we can live and serve without such affirmation from people. The Lord's affirmation and loving grace are sufficient for us. We follow him in humble and loving servanthood, as he himself came as the humble Servant (Matt. 20:28; Mark 10:45), obedient even to death on the cross for our salvation (see Phil. 2:5–11).

While we have been called to be servants of Jesus Christ (1 Cor. 4:1) and to follow him in the ministry of the towel (John 13:14–17), he has also called us to be his friends, not slaves or servants (John 15:15–17). The Lord Jesus has called us to servanthood that comes out of deep, loving, intimate friendship or communion with him. It is not servanthood out of obligation, duty, guilt, fear, or selfish motives for attention and praise, which is servitude. It is about serving our best friend. In doing so, we experience our deepest joy and fulfillment.

Servanthood, reflecting devoted discipleship, with a genuine Spirit-inspired servant attitude, is expressed in true service and not self-righteous service. Such servanthood, seasoned with suffering and humility, enables us to enter more deeply into God's rest and grace. It also revolutionizes our lives and ministries in the church, in the home, and in the workplace or school, producing fruit that will last for eternity as a result of the Holy Spirit's deep work.

This book explores servanthood and how to grow as true servants of our Lord and Savior, Jesus Christ. It will also paradoxically help those who have been called by God to leadership to become better leaders—as servants who serve in leadership.

I wish you the Lord's best and deepest blessings as you read on and grow in true servanthood in Christ.

1

Jesus' Call to Servanthood

Jesus Christ came to give us abundant and eternal life, or life to the full (John 10:10; 3:16). This kingdom life (Matt. 6:33) can only be fully experienced if we heed his call to discipleship in Luke 9:23: "If anyone would come after me, he must deny himself and take up his cross daily and follow me." The Lord Jesus has called all Christians, including Christian workers and leaders, to be his disciples by denying ourselves, taking up our cross daily, and following him all the way in obedience, even unto death if necessary (cf. Phil. 2:5–11).

A major part of such devoted discipleship is servanthood (Mark 10:42–45; cf. John 13:1–17). Servanthood is serving Jesus, or serving *with* Jesus, what Kortright Davis has called "servanting."[1] It involves not just being servants of Christ (1 Cor. 4:1) but being servants *with* Christ: servants in and through whom Christ lives and works, by the power of the Holy Spirit. It is servanthood with the right kind of servant attitude that comes from abiding in Christ (John 15:5) and following him in loving humility and caring compassion for the people we serve, for as servants of Christ we are also servants of people (2 Cor. 4:5). There is no preoccupation or even focus on greatness. As Lawrence Richards has put it: "Never a slave, with a bound will, Jesus freely chose to become a servant dedicated to act for the well-being of other[s] . . . (Matt. 20:28 and Luke 22:27). In Jesus' surrender of His life for our sakes, we see the ultimate servanthood, that of a free and uncoerced choice in which one places the good of others above oneself. . . . In our servanthood, we adopt the selfless attitude of Jesus . . . (1 Peter 4:10–11)."[2]

Jesus' own example as the Master Servant and his call to us to servanthood run contrary to the emphasis today on leadership and greatness. This emphasis is evident in both the secular world and the church. There is an ever-increasing amount of literature available on leadership and so-called Christian leadership. Similarly, leadership conferences for pastors and church leaders have been widely advertised and well-attended in recent years. In reading some of the leadership literature and attending several of these leadership conferences, I have become deeply concerned about the models of management and leadership that are often borrowed somewhat uncritically from the secular world. Such models tend to be applied too quickly to leadership in churches and parachurch organizations, without sufficient biblical reflection and critique. This topic will be dealt with in greater detail in a later chapter of this book. It is sufficient here to simply point out that Jesus has called us first to servanthood as his disciples, and not necessarily to leadership.

Steve Hayner, then president of InterVarsity Christian Fellowship USA, wrote a brief but excellent article in *World Vision Today* (Summer 1998) emphasizing this need for true servanthood rather than leadership. In his article, he wrote:

> There is a growing amount of modern literature on servant leadership. But I'm not sure I agree with leadership as the fundamental concept and servanthood as the modifier. Jesus gives an unmodified call to us to be servants—serving God and serving one another. Along the way, God may also call us into specific

roles of leadership. But there are no indications that obtaining those roles should be a believer's ultimate ambition. . . . Our ambition is not leadership, but servanthood. Our task is not to grow leaders, but to make disciples who will follow Jesus. Our goal is not to get out there and get things done, but to listen and obey. Our call is not to exercise power but to be faithful to our Lord and the way of the servant.

How God chooses to use his servants is his concern. We may be called to lead or to follow, to exert authority or to submit, to turn our God-given gifts in one direction or another. But that is God's business. Our identity, our meaning in life, our sense of significance, and our self-worth are not to be based on the roles we fill, the power we wield, or the numbers we lead. We play to an audience of one, who loves us, affirms us, and uses us. Whether we are called to perform the handstand or simply watch and clap from the sidelines, we should long to hear from our God the words, "Well done, you good and faithful servant!"[3]

The Ministry of the Towel: Footwashing Servanthood

In John 13:1–17, we read about Jesus' deeply touching example of footwashing servanthood. After he had finished washing the feet of his disciples as an act of humble, loving service, he said: "Now that I, your Lord and Teacher, have washed your feet, you also should wash one another's feet. I have set you an example that you should do as I have done for you. I tell you the truth, no servant is greater than his master, nor is a messenger greater than the one who sent him. Now that you know these things, you will be blessed if you do them" (John 13:14–17).

Jesus has called each of us as his disciple to follow his example of humble and loving footwashing servanthood to others. It is a call to the ministry of the towel, to true servanthood. While leadership and leadership development have their place in Christian ministry, servanthood is more foundational and central from a biblical perspective. God has called us first to servanthood (John 13:14–17; Mark 10:42–45; 1 Cor. 4:1), not leadership.

Servanthood, Not Greatness

In preparing to write this book, I came across a book on servanthood by David Cape and Tommy Tenney.[4] I was thrilled to learn about David Cape's Celebration of Servanthood seminars! I no longer have to say that there are leadership seminars and conferences galore but no seminars or conferences on servanthood. David, a former pastor, is also the founder of Footwasher Ministries. He has traveled widely, ministering the servant heart of Jesus to people ranging from world leaders and basketball stars to prostitutes and the forgotten and despised of this world. He has literally washed the feet of thousands of people across many nations! Tommy Tenney is well-known as a God chaser who pursues the heart of God and seeks to unite Christians from all denominations to minister together as God's humble servants.

Cape and Tenney have described the power of the towel, or the power of servanthood, in transforming thousands of lives for Jesus. They write about this as God's secret to greatness. Similarly, Bill Hybels, in an earlier book relevant to servanthood, wrote about descending into greatness,[5] meaning greatness in the sight of God, not human greatness. Hybels emphasized that such moving downward involves humility, brokenness, dependency, servanthood, and obedience. I understand their emphasis that true greatness lies in humble servanthood. Jesus said, "Not so with you. Instead whoever wants to become great among you must be your servant" (Mark 10:43). Yet, I believe Jesus' emphasis here is not so much on greatness, but on servanthood. Jesus was replying to the earlier request from James and John, the sons of Zebedee, to sit at his right and his left in his glory (Mark 10:35–37). Their preoccupation with greatness, and the Gentile world's obsession with leadership as exercising power and lording authority over others (Mark 10:42), were basically rebuked by Jesus. His answer: servanthood!

Similarly, when his disciples asked, "Who is the greatest in the kingdom of heaven?" Jesus called a little child and had him stand among them (Matt. 18:1–2). Jesus said to them: "I tell you the truth, unless you change and become like little children, you will never enter the kingdom of heaven. Therefore, whoever humbles himself like this child is the greatest in the kingdom of heaven" (Matt. 18:3–4). Jesus turned the disciples' misplaced concern with greatness to a focus on childlike humility. Jesus calls us to servanthood, pure and simple. He does not want us to be preoccupied or obsessed with greatness. In fact, trying to be great or to do great things for God can run counter to Christ-like servanthood. It was William Carey, "the Father of Modern Missions," who had as his watchword the now-famous statement: "Expect great things *from* God. Attempt great things *for* God." I believe he was trying to emphasize the greatness of God, not the greatness of human beings or the great things we can do for God. The real danger is that we can misunderstand Carey and misapply his watchword to read: "I want to do great things for God." This is often reduced to: "I want to be great and really count in God's kingdom!"

I am convinced that Jesus' call to servanthood can be more correctly translated to read: "I want to do things for a *great God*!" Whatever God who alone is great wants me to do, I'll do, with his help and the power of the Holy Spirit! This is simply obedience. Sometimes our great God may ask us to do *nothing* for a season: to be in solitude and deep communion with him alone. To simply "waste" time for God as Richard Foster would put it,[6] or what Marva Dawn would call "a royal waste of time" referring to the splendor of deep worship and communion with God.[7] But of course, it never is a waste of time when God calls us to a prolonged period in the wilderness to have more time with him in solitude and oftentimes silence. Sometimes our great

God may call us to do *little things* with great love, such as visiting shut-ins or bringing chicken soup to a neighbor who is ill. And sometimes our great God may call us to do big or so-called "*great" things* for him, such as to pastor and grow a church from 50 to 500 or 5,000!

Bruce Wilkinson recently wrote a story about how God calls us to leave the Land of Familiar to pursue our Big Dream and do great things for him.[8] He also tells real-life stories of miracles in his life and ministries in Africa that show how God will do great things in and through us for his glory, if we put him first: if we ask him what he wants done and then simply obey him, depending fully on the power of the Holy Spirit. Wilkinson challenges us to overcome the sin of unbelief and to trust God and believe that he can do the impossible in and through us. Sometimes God will call us to do great things for him. But he may also call us to do nothing, or little things with great love, for him. It takes as much trust or faith to obey him in doing nothing or little things as in doing great things. But it is all up to him. We simply obey, in true servanthood. Ultimately, servanthood is about following Jesus all the way, in loving and humble obedience. It is doing things for a great God.

Mother Teresa often emphasized that we can do no great things, only small things with great love. It is about servanthood, not greatness. It is about love and the God who is Love (1 John 4:8, 16). It is all about God, and not about us. God is God, and we are not! But paradoxically, as Rick Ferguson has pointed out, in servanthood or following the Servant Principle, we do find fulfillment through obedience to Christ.[9] In John Piper's well-known dictum: "God is most glorified in me when I am most satisfied in Him."[10] This happens in servanthood! We find our deepest joy, fulfillment, and satisfaction in him alone, in the one who has called us first to servanthood.

2

Learning from the Master Servant—Jesus

Jesus Christ is the Master Servant. The Gospel of Mark in particular portrays him as the Servant par excellence. We learn what true servanthood is all about from the Master Servant. Bruce Wilkinson in his daily devotional book, *Closer Walk*, succinctly summarizes the Gospel of Mark as focusing on Jesus the Servant:

> Writing to a Roman audience, Mark presents Jesus primarily as a servant, who ministers first as a servant to the crowds (Mark 1–7), then as a servant to the disciples (Mark 8–10), and finally as a servant to all humanity by giving His life as a ransom (Mark 11–16; see especially 10:45). In the final analysis, however, Jesus was a servant to His heavenly Father, sent forth to do His will.
>
> The call to service is rarely a call to convenience, and Jesus' life of servanthood was not easy. Note how Isaiah describes the role of the Servant-Messiah centuries before Jesus' birth (Isa. 52:13–53:12). Mark frequently describes the difficult life of the servant. You'll see Jesus interrupted as He spends time in prayer. You'll

> feel the eager crowds pressing in to tap His power. You'll sense His compassion for those in need and His anger at those using traditions as an excuse to avoid serving others. And you'll sense His resolute commitment to face the cross in spite of its agony and shame. Truly Jesus is the supreme model of servanthood.
>
> Your call as a disciple is likewise a call to servanthood. Do you place your Master's will ahead of your own? Does your heart respond with compassion at the sight of needy people? Do your actions speak louder than words? Active, compassionate, obedient service to the Master—that's your joyful privilege today and everyday. Are you ready to enter the Savior's school of servanthood?[1]

Indeed the Savior has called us to enter his school of servanthood: to follow him, the Master Servant, all the way. Besides the Gospel of Mark, there are several other New Testament passages that contain Jesus' words on servanthood (e.g., Matt. 20:28; Luke 22:26–27) and his own example of servanthood (e.g., John 13:14–17; Phil. 2:5–11). We have already referred to Jesus' example of footwashing servanthood in John 13:14–17 in the previous chapter. A key text in the Bible we need to consider more carefully is Philippians 2:5–11:

> Your attitude should be the same as that of Christ Jesus:
> Who, being in very nature God,
> did not consider equality with God something to be grasped,
> but made himself nothing,
> taking the very nature of a servant,
> being made in human likeness.
> And being found in appearance as a man,
> he humbled himself
> and became obedient to death—even death on a cross!
> Therefore God exalted him to the highest place
> and gave him the name that is above every name,
> that at the name of Jesus every knee should bow,
> in heaven and on earth and under the earth,

> and every tongue confess that Jesus Christ is Lord,
> to the glory of the Father.

This text is often quoted, rightfully so, as a description of the supreme example of servanthood shown by the Master Servant himself, Jesus. We often conclude that Paul is here teaching us to follow Jesus' example of servanthood, by trying to imitate and be like him, as his servants. Upon deeper reflection, and following more careful scholarship and interpretation of this text, we see that this is not quite what Paul is saying in Philippians 2:5–11. Ralph Martin, renowned New Testament scholar, has written a substantial book on Philippians 2:5–11 as a hymn of Christ, in the setting of early Christian worship, as well as in recent interpretation of this text by Bible scholars. He notes that these verses in Philippians have actually been difficult and baffling to interpret.

Martin points out that Philippians 2:5 can be more accurately translated as: "Act as befits those who are in Christ Jesus" (rather than "Let this mind be in you which was also in Christ Jesus" as the Authorized Version puts it). Martin goes on to write: "The Lord's name is used as a pendant to what follows, and not as the introduction of a portrait of His character and actions which are meant to be imitated. . . . The controlling motive of Pauline ethics is not imitation, but death and resurrection. It involves a death to sin in baptism and a sharing of His risen life in the Spirit."[2] Martin then makes the following conclusion about Philippians 2:5b:

> Paul is summoning the Philippians to act in such a way as befits their standing in Christ Jesus, i.e., as members of His church. He is reminding them of what they should be as those who are "in Him." . . . He is saying in effect: This is how you came to be incorporated into Christ . . . and you are "in Him"; and, as such, you are called to live a life which has His redeeming acts as its foundation. . . . The Apostolic summons is not: Follow Jesus by

> doing what He did—an impossible feat in any case, for who can be a "second Christ" who quits His heavenly glory and dies in shame and is taken up into the throne of the universe? The appeal and injunction to the Philippians in their pride and selfishness are rather: Become in your conduct and church relationships the type of persons who, by that *kenosis*, death and exaltation of the Lord of glory, have a place in His body, the church.[3]

Pulling all of this together, we can now see more clearly that Paul is telling us in this passage to be who we really are "in Christ." We learn from Jesus himself to follow him by remaining or abiding in him (cf. John 15:5), fully dependent on him. We do not try to be like him. Instead, we walk with him daily and continue to be "in him," in our intimate, loving relationship with him. As we continue to develop and grow deeper in this "transforming friendship"[4] with the Lord, our lives will be changed and transformed more and more into his likeness, by the power and presence of the Holy Spirit (2 Cor. 3:18). What we learn from Jesus is precisely what he says in John 15:5: Without him, we can do absolutely nothing! Servanthood Jesus' style is therefore not trying to imitate or be like him. It is letting *him* transform us and make us more like him, by the power of the Holy Spirit because of his death and resurrection for us. It is not by might or by power or by self-effort—it is by his Spirit, with supernatural power from above (Zech. 4:6).

Some years ago, there was a widespread movement amongst grassroots Christians worldwide to imitate Jesus by asking the WWJD question: *What Would Jesus Do*? After trying to answer this question in a specific area or context of life, many then tried to do what they thought Jesus would do. And many failed! One pastor a few years ago actually changed WWJD to read: *What Would Jesus Drive*? He was absolutely sure that Jesus would never drive an SUV because of the terrible ecological consequences to the environment due to the low gas mileage obtained! Yet another well-known pastor was sure Jesus would drive an SUV! Such questions only cause confusion.

We cannot become more like Jesus by self-effort or sheer imitation of Christ. We will fail. But we can follow another WWJD: Walking with Jesus Daily. We can, with the help and empowering of the Holy Spirit, walk with Jesus daily by spending time with him in prayer, Bible reading and meditation, worship, solitude and silence, and other spiritual disciplines.[5] As we abide or remain in him in the sweet communion of his transforming friendship, he will change us and mold us to become more like him. It is the Holy Spirit (Eph. 5:18; 2 Cor. 3:18) who will transform us, conforming us into the image of Christ (Rom. 8:29), or forming Christ in us (Gal. 4:19).

Servanthood, or following Jesus all the way, therefore, means that we live in Jesus all the way. We follow him by letting him lead us and take full control of our lives. We follow him by remaining or abiding in him (John 15:5) and thereby bearing much fruit that will remain for eternity. We thus serve our best friend, Jesus! Friendship with Christ is the topic of our next chapter. It is also the secret of true servanthood.

3

Serving Our Best Friend

The secret of true servanthood is friendship with Jesus, our best friend. In John 15:15–17, Jesus says:

> I no longer call you servants, because a servant does not know his master's business. Instead, I have called you friends, for everything that I learned from my Father I have made known to you. You did not choose me, but I chose you to go and bear fruit—fruit that will last. Then the Father will give you whatever you ask in my name. This is my command: Love each other.

Jesus makes it clear in this text that he calls us his friends, no longer servants or slaves. Edward Zaragoza uses this text to advocate a new paradigm or model for ordained ministry centered on friendship with Jesus and each other based on compassion and love. He strongly criticizes servanthood and servant-leadership as inadequate and unhelpful models for ministry. "No longer servants, but friends" is the biblical paradigm for ministry according to Zaragoza.[1] While I agree with Zaragoza that friendship with Jesus, and loving and compassionate friendship with each other, should be the biblical foundations of our ministry or service, I believe that Jesus still calls us to servanthood. The foot-washing servanthood he taught and modeled for us in John 13:1–17 is not negated by what he says in John 15:15–17. When Jesus calls us friends and no longer servants or slaves, he says to each of us: "Your fundamental, core identity is as a friend of mine. You are not fundamentally or essentially a slave or servant. You are my friend. Out of this special, loving intimate friendship with me, I have called you to go in true servanthood with me, empowering you by the Holy Spirit to bear fruit—fruit that will last for eternity!"

Our core identity is therefore as friends of Jesus. He has called and chosen us to enter into the deep, loving community of the Trinity: Father, Son, and Holy Spirit. We are no longer slaves or servants at the core of our being, because Jesus has revealed everything he learned from the Father to us. We have been drawn into the inner circle of God himself. This is an awesome and life-transforming truth, what James Houston calls "the transforming friendship" with God. However, out of this friendship, we still serve our best friend in true servanthood anointed by the power of the Holy Spirit. Friendship with the Lord, our best friend, founded on prayer and intimate communion with him, is the foundation of true servanthood. It does *not* replace servanthood as Zaragoza erroneously asserts. True servanthood based on friendship with Jesus is *not* servanthood out of obligation, duty, guilt, fear, or selfish motives for attention and praise. It is *not* the "doormat" servitude Zaragoza criticizes as unbiblical, which will receive further treatment in the next chapter. The rest of this chapter will focus on how to develop our friendship with Jesus; how to know him more as our best friend, so that in true servanthood we will be serving our best friend.

Walking with Jesus Daily

Our friendship with Jesus can be described as Walking with Jesus Daily, or WWJD now correctly interpreted. In recent years, several authors have written about the spiritual disciplines as a means to grow into deeper intimacy with God in our friendship with Jesus. Spiritual disciplines, according to Dallas Willard, "refer to an ancient tradition of activities which are means of grace, ways of approaching and relating richly to God . . . activities in our power, things that we can do, to meet God in such a way that we become able to do what we cannot do by direct effort."[2] Such disciplines have been part of Christian tradition since very early on (see, e.g., 1 Cor. 9:27; 1 Tim. 4:7–8). Willard describes two major categories of spiritual disciplines: *disciplines of abstinence* (solitude, silence, fasting, frugality, chastity, secrecy, and sacrifice), and *disciplines of engagement* (study, worship, celebration, service, prayer, fellowship, confession, and submission).[3]

Richard Foster wrote the classic book *Celebration of Discipline* (originally in 1978) that sparked a revival of interest in the spiritual disciplines as means of God's grace for spiritual growth in Christ and into greater Christlikeness. Foster proposed the following categories: the *inward disciplines* of meditation, prayer, fasting, and study; the *outward disciplines* of simplicity, solitude, submission, and service; and the *corporate disciplines* of confession, worship, guidance, and celebration.[4]

More recently in *Disciplines of the Holy Spirit*, Douglas Gregg and I described the following spiritual disciplines as power connectors to the presence and power of the Holy Spirit, who enables us to grow in our friendship with Jesus and to become more and more like him: "Drawing Near to God: Disciplines of Solitude" (solitude and silence, listening and guidance, prayer and intercession, study and meditation); "Yielding to God: Disciplines of Surrender" (repentance and confession, yielding and submission, fasting, and worship); "Reaching Out to

Others: Disciplines of Service" (fellowship, simplicity, service, and witness).[5]

In other books, the list of disciplines varies from author to author.[6] However, all of the disciplines refer to spiritual practices or activities that help us grow in our friendship with Jesus, to become more mature in him and more like him. It is important to realize however that we need the Holy Spirit's presence and power even in the *practice* of the spiritual disciplines! For example, there are times when we want but are unable to pray or read the Bible or fast. We need to ask the Holy Spirit to empower us to practice the disciplines themselves and not just to help us, through the disciplines, to eventually do what we cannot do on our own, such as giving generously and sacrificially or loving our enemies. In this sense then, the spiritual disciplines are not simply what we can do, or activities in our power. We often fail in our own power to practice them. We need the help and empowering of the Holy Spirit even in the very practice of the spiritual disciplines, and as we do so we are empowered even more by him to do what we cannot do: To become more like Jesus and to grow in our friendship with him.

The spiritual disciplines are nothing in and of themselves. They are potentially dangerous; they can become legalistic self-efforts at trying to please God or impress him to bless us. They are really means of grace, God's loving invitation to enter into deeper intimacy with him. The disciplines simply enable us to create more time and space for God. God has to work and touch us first.

The Secret of Transforming Power in Jesus' Life

While all the spiritual disciplines are important for developing a well-balanced and full-orbed spiritually mature life in Christ, I would like to focus on the disciplines that were crucial in Jesus' own life and ministry.

In the midst of his busy ministry, meeting the needs of many people, Jesus regularly took time off to be in solitude and to pray, to be in communion with the Father by the power of the Holy Spirit (Matt. 14:23; 26:36; Mark 1:35; 6:46; 14:32; Luke 5:16; 6:12; 22:41; John 17:1; Heb. 5:7). This was the secret of transforming power in Jesus' life and ministry. It is also the secret of transforming power for us in our lives and ministries.

Just as Jesus spent regular time in prayer, in solitude and silence, in communion with the Father, so must we if we are to develop a deeper friendship with Jesus and love relationship with God himself. And so must we if we are to serve Jesus with the transforming power of the Holy Spirit to lovingly touch lives forever, to bear fruit that will last for eternity. It is about abiding in Christ or remaining in friendship and communion with him (John 15:5), thereby bearing much fruit. Without him, apart from him, we can do nothing.

Richard Foster, in another classic book, wrote the following deeply moving words on the heart of God for each one of us:

> God has graciously allowed me to catch a glimpse into his heart, and I want to share with you what I have seen. Today the heart of God is an open wound of love. He aches over our distance and preoccupation. He mourns that we do not draw near to him. He grieves that we have forgotten him. He weeps over our obsession with muchness and manyness. He longs for our presence.
>
> And he is inviting you—and me—to come home, to come home where we belong, to come home to that for which we were created. His arms are stretched out wide to receive us. His heart is enlarged to take us in.
>
> For too long we have been in a far country: a country of noise and hurry and crowds, a country of climb and push and shove, a country of frustration and fear and intimidation. And he welcomes us home: home to friendship and fellowship and openness, home to intimacy and acceptance and affirmation.
>
> The key to this home, this heart of God, is prayer.[7]

Following our best friend's example, we need to take time to pray: time to be in solitude and silence and in deep, loving communion with God in response to his longing and radical love for us. We can do this in a daily quiet time with the Lord, in prayer, silence, Bible reading, and meditation on Scripture. We need to remember that this is a quiet time, whether for fifteen minutes or an hour or more, spent in deep fellowship and friendship with our best friend. A daily quiet time with the Lord cannot be rushed or hurried. When I was a young Christian, I was taught to "do" my quiet time each day with the following structure or schedule: pray, read the Bible, pray. Now I realize that daily quiet time is time to "be" with the Lord rather than to "do" an activity or spiritual practice. It must include quiet or silence in waiting upon him and hearing his loving, still small voice or gentle whisper (1 Kings 19:11–13). My revised structure for a quiet time with the Lord now includes: be quiet (in silence), pray, be quiet, read the Bible, be quiet, pray, be quiet, pray. Being quiet is a big part of a daily quiet time with the Lord. Being quiet, or silent, is part of contemplative prayer.

In addition to a daily quiet time, we should take a more prolonged retreat time with the Lord, for 24 to 48 hours or more, at least once a year. Emilie Griffin has written a helpful guide for having such personal spiritual retreat, or wilderness time, that will greatly enrich our friendship with Jesus.[8] We may initially experience restlessness, hunger, and sleepiness during a prolonged private retreat with the Lord.[9] If so, we need only allow ourselves to walk with Jesus around the retreat grounds to overcome our restlessness, eat something to overcome our hunger, and sleep and fully rest in the Lord to fulfill our sleepiness. There'll be ample time later to pray, fast, and be still and awake before the Lord!

Finally, we need to be in an attitude of prayer throughout the day, to "pray continually" (1 Thess. 5:17), to "pray in the Spirit on all occasions with all kinds of prayers and requests" (Eph. 6:18). We can do this by sending up short prayers to God throughout the day; "practicing the presence of God" as Brother Lawrence would put it, in all that we do, everywhere we are. This is truly Walking with Jesus Daily, moment by moment! The Bible also calls this walking in the Spirit or keeping in step with the Holy Spirit (Gal. 5:25), yielding to his control moment by moment, and thus being continually filled with the Spirit (Eph. 5:18). It is experiencing life in the Spirit (John 16:13–15; Rom. 8:9–17, 26–27; 1 Cor. 2:6–16; Gal. 5:16, 25).

Gary Moon has described friendship with Jesus as falling for God or saying Yes to his extravagant proposal to enter into a deep, loving intimacy with him. He notes however: "It is far too easy to become distracted from our journey into intimacy with God. Sometimes heady questions get in the way. What would Jesus do? or eat? or think? Would Jesus buy an Oldsmobile or a Toyota? Would he drink Pepsi or wine? Would he think about politics or religion? Who knows? Are these the questions we should be asking? I don't think so, because they allow us to appreciate Jesus from a distance, or as a belief system, instead of as a live-in-twenty-four-hour-a-day intimate friend. The better question, the real question is: How will I *be* as Jesus lives his life through me?"[10]

Moon also describes the three Cs of falling for God: conversation, communion, and consummation (or union), each in ever deepening intimacy with God, ending up in consummation or union with him. Falling for God radically involves surrender to him. Moon has pointed out that such surrender hurts, but it is the sweet ache of letting go![11] Ultimately, however, it is "a surrender to Love" which is the heart of Christian spirituality as David Benner puts it.[12]

God is crazily and deeply in love with us! He longs for us. He is deeply touched when we long for him and fall madly in love with him in response to his radical and extravagant love for us. In Zephaniah 3:17, we read: "The LORD your God is with you, he is mighty to save. He will take great delight in you, he will quiet you with his love, he will rejoice over you with singing."

Ultimately, it is about God and being in love with him because he loved us first (1 John 4:19). It is about being alive in Christ and about Jesus and our friendship with him. It is not about spiritual disciplines. Paul makes this crystal clear in Galatians 2:20: "I have been crucified with Christ and I no longer live, but Christ lives in me. The life I live in the body, I live by faith in the Son of God, who loved me and gave himself for me."

We live our lives and serve in our ministries by faith or trust in Jesus, the Son of God and our best friend. Friendship with Jesus will lead us ultimately into friendship with the Triune God—Father, Son, and Holy Spirit in the eternal community of the Trinity.

Just Give Me Jesus and More of Jesus

Anne Graham Lotz, the daughter of Billy and Ruth Bell Graham, told the following story of her life a few years ago in her book, *Just Give Me Jesus*:

> My life during the past two years has been pressure packed and trouble filled. My husband's dental office, where he had practiced for thirty years, burned to the ground. All three of my children got married within eight months of each other. My son was diagnosed with cancer and went through successful surgery and follow-up radiation. I published two books, *God's Story* and *Daily Light*, as well as *The Daily Light Journal: Morning Readings*. I produced a seven-volume video series with workbooks and study guides for *The Vision of His Glory*. I kept up an intense speaking schedule that included international travel, fulfilled ministry obligations, and gave physical care to my parents including going through my mother's five emergency hospitalizations within a span of ten months. My ministry, AnGeL Ministries, is currently going

> through a transition that has increased our yearly budget six fold. . . .
>
> My duties and responsibilities at times seem overwhelming and my schedule is overfilled. But I don't want a vacation, I don't want to quit, I don't want sympathy, I don't want money, I don't want recognition, I don't want escape, I don't even want a miracle! This book is the cry of my heart—just give me Jesus. Please![13]

Anne Graham Lotz's longing and passion for Jesus is obvious. Her heart's cry is for a deeper and more intimate friendship with Jesus. This is the secret foundation of her servanthood: she is serving her best friend.

In a subsequent book, *My Heart's Cry*, she expressed a longing for more of Jesus, because when you love someone with all of your heart, you just can't get enough! Her heart's cry is "Just give me more of Jesus!" in the following areas: more of his voice in my ear, more of his tears on my face, more of his praise on my lips, more of his death in my life, more of his dirt on my hands, more of his hope in my grief, more of his fruit in my service, more of his love in my home, more of his courage in my convictions, more of his nearness in my loneliness, more of his answers to my prayers, and more of his glory on my knees.[14]

In my own daily walk with Jesus in over thirty-seven years now as a Christian (I came to know Jesus as my personal Lord and Savior on August 12, 1968, in Singapore, my country of origin), my daily quiet time with him has been a crucial, foundational part of my friendship with him. He is my best friend. And through Jesus, I have come to know the Triune God—Father, Son, and Holy Spirit—as my best friend, having been drawn into the eternal community of love, the eternal community of the Trinity. What an awesome privilege and experience! "What a Friend We Have in Jesus" as the hymn says! And out of this deep, intimate, loving friendship, with him and in him, he has led me, by the power of the Holy Spirit, into true servanthood in loving ministry to others. I am serving my best friend who loves me more than

I can ever realize this side of the kingdom. My ultimate identity is as a friend of Jesus, a friend of God, and a beloved child of God (John 1:12). True servanthood is not slavery to others or doormat servitude. True servanthood is relational. It starts with passionately longing for and loving Jesus with full surrender, or the sweet ache of letting go. There is deep joy, comfort, and fulfillment in knowing Jesus so intimately. True servanthood is founded on deep friendship with Jesus: Walking with Jesus Daily. True servanthood is all about serving our best friend.

4

Servanthood Versus Servitude

Serving our best friend Jesus is what true servanthood is all about. It is very different from doormat servitude or slavery to other people's demands and wants. Kenneth Haugk, the founder of the Stephen's Series of lay caring ministry, has helpfully differentiated servanthood from servitude. He points out that servitude is associated with "bondage, slavery, and involuntary labor" whereas servanthood is characterized more by "willingness, choice, and voluntary commitment."[1]

According to Haugk, there are four basic problems with servitude. First is *overidentification*, taking on the problems of the other (the person you are ministering to) at the expense of losing your own identity. Second is *superficial sweetness and gushiness*, compensating for anger or frustration by covering up feelings. Third is *being manipulated*, allowing the other to abuse your relationship or take advantage of you. Fourth and finally is *begrudging care*, complaining about your caregiving relationships, often with feelings of resentment and frustration.[2]

Haugk also describes four corresponding responses of servanthood that are more appropriate and healthy. First is *empathy*, feeling with the other (the person you are ministering to or helping) while retaining good objectivity and maintaining your own identity. Second is *genuineness*, being yourself, with your own wounds and all, and acting congruently. Third is *meeting needs, not wants*, which is being straightforward about your feelings, speaking the truth in love, and confronting another when necessary. Fourth and finally is *intentionality*, choosing to be in a caregiving relationship, or getting out of it when that is the best option for all concerned.[3]

As I have previously written, "servanthood is not being a doormat for everyone to walk over and abuse or manipulate, with an inability to say no to unreasonable requests, or worse still, vicious demands. Servanthood flows out of obedience to God's will, out of deep friendship and communion with the Lord, who will guide us at times to lay down our lives and sacrifice for others, and at other times to say no without feeling guilty. In true servanthood, then, we give up control to the Lord our Master and not to people."[4]

I clearly recall an example from my own life and ministry that helps illustrate the difference between servitude and servanthood as I have described and as Haugk has clarified. Quite a number of years ago while I was living and working in Toronto, Ontario, I received a pleasant phone call from one of the leaders and organizers of an upcoming Christian conference. I was asked if I would accept their invitation to speak to their small group Bible study leaders. When I found out that they wanted me to speak on a Sunday morning, I politely told them no because I had to preach that Sunday afternoon in my church where I was serving as the part-time pastor. I felt I needed the time on Sunday morning to pray and prepare to preach later that afternoon at our worship service which regularly met on Sunday afternoons. The person who had invited me was deeply disappointed and ended up telling me that if *I really* wanted to serve them and speak as requested, I would say yes and accept their invitation since it was for Sunday morning and hence would not directly clash with my preaching that Sunday afternoon. Fortunately, I was able to see through this attempt at guilt manipulation and stuck to my saying no politely and more firmly this time. In true servanthood, the Lord led me and enabled me to say no. In servitude I would have said yes, giving in to an unreasonable demand and guilt manipulation, and trying to please others and meet all their requests and demands. My church would have suffered and so would I if I had accepted the invitation. I would have risked taking on too much and being hurried and harried, if not burned out!

However, I should point out that at other times the Lord may call us in true servanthood to lay down our lives and to sacrifice for others. I recall my experience on a preaching/ministry trip several years ago. After a full schedule of preaching and speaking each day for several days, I was being driven to the airport in a van with several other friends. I was tired but deeply thankful to the Lord for blessing and touching so many lives on this trip. A friend asked me to speak with another person in the van who needed to talk about some family issues, and who wanted my counsel and prayer ministry. My immediate reaction was a negative one. I felt upset at my friend for being so insensitive to my tiredness and need for rest on the way to the airport. However, the Lord helped me to release this negative reaction and filled me afresh with his love. The Holy Spirit then empowered me to sacrificially serve and minister to this person.

Misunderstanding Servanthood

As mentioned in the previous chapter, Edward Zaragoza, a seminary professor, has written a strong critique of both servanthood and servant leadership. He instead advocates friendship as the correct, biblical model for ordained ministry.[5]

In his criticism of servanthood as a paradigm for ministry, Zaragoza reviews and summarizes three major contemporary critiques of servanthood, written by women theologians. The first contemporary critique of servanthood is from *Beyond Servanthood: Christianity and the Liberation of Women*, by feminist theologian Susan Nelson Dunfee. Dunfee calls women to wholeness and freedom. She argues that servanthood, typically understood and described, promotes the second-class status of women and results in a dependency between the woman and those she serves because she is to be "selfless" in servanthood. Instead, she advocates friendship as the new model for calling women to freedom and wholeness based on what Jesus said in John 15:15.[6]

The second contemporary critique of servanthood Zaragoza covers is from an article written by Jacquelyn Grant, a womanist theologian. Grant believes that African-American women in particular need to be empowered. Servanthood language has not helped to empower them. Instead it has hidden the real servitude of these women and led to the perpetuation of systems of suffering and oppression for them. She suggests "discipleship" as "a more meaningful way of speaking about the life-work of Christians."[7]

The third and final contemporary critique of servanthood Zaragoza mentions is from an article by Ada María Isasi-Díaz, a mujerista theologian. She discusses the "no greater love" text in the Gospel of John that has so frequently been used as the ultimate expression of servanthood. Although she does not directly refer to servanthood, she describes the Latina word of *lucha*, or struggle, that has many similarities to servanthood. Zaragoza summarizes Isasi-Díaz's views thus: "In short, no greater love is not about death but about life with justice. . . . Justice is the end of oppression in a Latina's daily struggle with exploitation, marginalization, powerlessness, cultural imperialism, and systemic violence. . . . Isasi-Díaz goes a step further in her article by calling for the oppressor and the oppressed to come together in a solidarity to undo oppressive systems. This relationship is one of mutuality. Isasi-Díaz calls it friendship. Each side of the friendship empowers the other, and this empowerment creates the power to transform society."[8]

After reviewing and summarizing these three contemporary critiques of servanthood by women theologians, Zaragoza himself makes the following conclusions:

> We have forgotten that our real service is worship. With its focus on the person rather than God, the paradigm of servanthood that is presented to seminary students and pastors wrongly values the individual instead of the community, doing over being, giving up power instead of empowerment, adversity (being adversarial) rather than friendship as formative, and heroic struggle as more important than the daily struggle for survival. The effects of such a paradigm make us less than we are because we spend so much time and effort trying to be more than we can be.[9]

I have gone into some detail to present Zaragoza's critique of servanthood because it is an important contemporary view. While I agree with some of the criticisms raised about the *concept* of servanthood as he and others have described, I believe that Zaragoza is criticizing *servitude* or some other sub-biblical or unbiblical idea of servanthood, and not true servanthood that is fully biblical. "Misunderstanding servanthood" would be a good way to respond to Zaragoza and others who want to do away with the concept of servanthood altogether. They have thrown out the baby with the bathwater so to speak! True servanthood, when properly understood and biblically clarified, is a central and essential teaching from Scripture. It is also a substantial part of *discipleship*, which is a more comprehensive biblical term referring to our living in Jesus and following him all the way.

Understanding True Servanthood

True servanthood flows out of a deep friendship with Jesus. True servanthood is empowered by the Holy Spirit as a result of abiding or remaining in Christ (John 15:5), producing spiritual, eternal fruit in becoming more like Jesus and touching many lives for Jesus by drawing people to him. True servanthood is characterized by loving obedience to the Lord, and compassionate ministry to others. True servanthood fulfills our deepest longings and calling. It does not diminish us or others, except to die to our sinful, false self. True servanthood enables us to grow up mature and real in Christ, with authenticity. True servanthood is not about imitating Jesus or trying to be like him through our own self-efforts. It is about living in Jesus and Jesus living in us by the power of the Holy Spirit. It is about Jesus then living through us to reach out to a broken world with love and friendship, centered in our loving friendship with him first. True servanthood focuses on God and not the individual.

Zaragoza's negative description of servanthood is actually more of a critique of unbiblical servitude than of true, biblical servanthood. Servitude or some other erroneous concept of servanthood therefore values the individual over community, doing over being, giving up power instead of empowerment, being adversarial (adversity) rather than friendship as formative, and heroic struggle as more important than the daily struggle for survival. True servanthood that is biblical and Christlike values the community as well as the individual, being over doing, giving up power as well as empowerment, friendship and not being adversarial or competitive, and the daily struggle for survival but occasionally also "heroic" struggle, if by that is meant sometimes being persecuted for our faith in Christ and even dying for him!

True servanthood results in true service whereas servitude or some other sub-biblical or unbiblical form of "servanthood" results in self-righteous service, which is closer to what Zaragoza and others have criticized. True service versus self-righteous service will be covered in more detail in chapter 6.

We do not have to give up on the concept of servanthood. This beautiful concept refers to our call from the Lord to be his friends first and then to go out in true servanthood to minister to a broken world. True servants also humbly and lovingly acknowledge their own brokenness, as "wounded healers" themselves. It is servanthood that Jesus has called us to, not servitude!

5

Servanthood Versus Servant Leadership

This chapter is probably the most difficult for me to write. To deal with the huge topic of leadership in a single chapter is already difficult and near impossible enough. To do so from the perspective of true servanthood is even more difficult and just about impossible! However, I believe that this is a necessary chapter. So much that has been written and advocated in the area of leadership needs further biblical reflection and critique. Especially the concept and model so often used for leadership in Christian circles: servant leadership. Servant leadership has been both too quickly criticized and too quickly embraced.

Servant Leadership

As we saw in the previous chapter, Edward Zaragoza has strongly criticized servanthood in a way that I believe reflects his misunderstanding of true, biblical servanthood. He has even more strongly criticized the concept and model of servant leadership. Servant leadership was first coined by Robert K. Greenleaf in his seminal 1970 essay, "The Servant as Leader" and then described further in 1977 in a now widely read and known book, *Servant Leadership: A Journey into the Nature of Legitimate Power and Greatness*. He emphasized that servant leaders are servants first. In serving others, they should ask the following crucial questions: "Do those served grow as persons? Do they, while being served, become healthier, wiser, freer, more autonomous, more likely themselves to become servants? And what is the effect on the least privileged in society; will they benefit, or at least, not be further deprived?"[1]

In a subsequent book, Greenleaf again underscored the need for leaders to be servants first. He wrote that the servant leader "is sharply different from the person who is leader first. . . . The difference manifests itself in the care taken by the servant—first to make sure that other people's highest priority needs are being served."[2] Greenleaf also advocated that more servants should emerge as leaders or should follow only servant leaders. Zaragoza cites these two famous passages from Greenleaf's most influential writings but notes that they are not as biblically based as many Christians think they are.[3]

In fact, Greenleaf originally got his inspiration for servant leadership from a novel entitled *Journey to the East* (New York: Noonday Press, 1956) written by Herman Hesse, and not directly from Scripture. However, Greenleaf did describe what to him is a great illustration of servant leadership based on the story of Jesus and the adulterous woman, found in John 7:53–8:11.[4] Zaragoza notes that Greenleaf used this story to illustrate what a servant leader does: "He has a vision or goal, devises a plan that will realize that vision, and then puts that plan into action, thereby achieving the goal."[5] He criticizes such a concept of servant leadership because it emphasizes individualism, having extraordinary or profound vision, and maintaining one's own leadership by being competitive and winning or staying in control of a person or situation.[6]

Zaragoza makes the following conclusions about Greenleaf's concept of servant leadership: "The emphasis in Greenleaf is not Jesus' earthly ministry, but on a generic brand of 'indispensable' servant leadership. Remember, Jesus is just one example of an effective servant leader. If Greenleaf was really interested in promoting a life that imitates Christ, then he would be arguing for the servanthood of Jesus as a paradigm, not servant leadership. Servant leadership is not the same as servanthood. In spite of the adjective servant, servant leadership draws the church toward business paradigms, not toward Christocentric ones."[7] He further states that Greenleaf's "servant leader is really a corporate CEO in disguise! Greenleaf's emphasis is really on the leadership abilities of the person and not on the followers. . . . It is dangerous to impose the standard of servant leadership on the church. . . . Therefore, as a paradigm, servant leadership sets forth a governing pattern or framework by which ministry is interpreted as leadership first, and then servanthood. In so doing, servant leadership offers a very troubling misreading of Jesus."[8]

Zaragoza also specifically critiques three books on church leadership that are based on servant leadership, pointing out that the authors tend to confuse servant leadership with servanthood. The first book, written by Ray S. Anderson, former professor of theology and ministry at Fuller Theological Seminary, emphasized that servant leaders are not doormats and that the pastor is not the servant of people but the servant of God. The second book by Bennett J. Sims, a retired Episcopal bishop, emphasized that servant leaders do not control. Sims also focused on great leadership as centered in the ability to empower others and hence is really servanthood. Finally, the third book, by Celia Hahn, a Christian educator, emphasized that servant leaders do what's needed, by being servants to one another through love and discovering that they have what it takes to do what is needed.[9]

There are many other books founded on the concept and model of servant leadership. For example, Calvin Miller wrote: "the number one quality that must mark tomorrow's leaders is servanthood. . . . But this servanthood will have to couple with other far-ranging executive qualities as well. We cannot set a date out there when we will begin promoting servanthood as a leadership style. This kind of leadership is nurtured in the Spirit by following Jesus. Servant leaders generally are created not in commanding others but in obeying their Commander. In such a mystique, executive arrogance is not possible. The yielded leader is always an incarnation of Christ, the real leader of His church."[10]

Similarly, Max De Pree, well-known and deeply respected author on leadership and chairman emeritus of Herman Miller, Inc., stated: "*The servanthood of leadership* needs to be felt, understood, believed and practiced if we're to be faithful. The best description of this kind of leadership is found in the book of Luke: 'The greatest among you should be like the youngest, and the one who rules like the one who serves.' The finest instruction in how to practice it can be found in *Servant Leadership* by Robert Greenleaf, a lovely grace note to the melody in Luke."[11] In another book, De Pree wrote: "The first responsibility of a leader is to define reality. The last is to say thank you. In between the two, the leader must become a servant and a debtor. That sums up the progress of an artful leader."[12] Again, we see the terms servanthood and servant leadership used somewhat interchangeably and synonymously, as if they mean the same thing. They in fact do not mean the same thing, and this confusion has already been pointed out by Zaragoza.

Servanthood Versus Servant Leadership

Zaragoza has some valid criticisms of servant leadership. If servanthood is practiced only to serve the purposes and goals of leadership, and hence leadership precedes servanthood, in so-called servant leadership, then this kind of servant leadership is not biblical. However, Zaragoza's description of such servant leadership is biased toward the negative. Nor is he always accurate in his criticisms of Greenleaf's concept of servant leadership. Greenleaf specifically points out that leaders must be servants first. Zaragoza describes servant leadership as leadership first and then servanthood. Although this is not fully correct, he does accurately discern the tendency for the hidden agenda or emphasis in servant leadership to still be on the leader and his or her vision and the fulfillment of that vision. This is why as mentioned earlier in this book, Steve Hayner wrote: "There is a growing amount of modern literature on servant leadership. But I'm not sure if I agree with leadership as the fundamental concept and servanthood as the modifier. Jesus gives an unmodified call to us to be servants—serving God and serving one another."[13]

Servant leadership can therefore be seen as an oxymoron. It is often used in a confusing way that includes servanthood. But servanthood is not the same as servant leadership. As Rick Warren has pointed out in *The Purpose-Driven Life*: "Thousands of books have been written on leadership, but few on servanthood. Everyone wants to lead; no one wants to be a servant. We would rather be generals than privates. Even Christians want to be '*servant-leaders,*' not just plain servants. But to be like Jesus is to be a servant. That's what he called himself. . . . It is possible to serve in church for a lifetime without ever being a servant. You must have a servant's heart."[14]

Warren goes on to describe the following characteristics of real servants who have a servant's heart: they make themselves available to serve; they pay attention to needs; they do their best with what they have; they do every task with equal dedication; they are faithful to their ministry; and they maintain a low profile.[15] He also emphasizes that real servants have a mind-set with the following five attitudes: they think more about others than about themselves; they think like stewards, not owners (knowing that

God owns it all); they think about their work, not what others are doing; they base their identity in Christ; and they think of ministry as an opportunity, not an obligation.[16]

Servanthood must always come first. Leadership is a secondary calling that God may give to some of us. All of us, however, have been called to servanthood as devoted disciples of Jesus Christ. While the concept of servant leadership can be criticized, some authors have used it to refer to a leadership style or approach that has servanthood or a servant's heart as its foundation. Larry Spears, in *Reflections on Leadership*, emphasizes again Greenleaf's belief that a servant-leader is a servant first. Spears wrote: "At its core, servant-leadership is a long-term, transformational approach to life and work, in essence, a way of being that has potential to create positive change throughout our society."[17] He then identified the following ten critical characteristics of the servant-leader: listening, empathy, healing, awareness, persuasion, conceptualization, foresight, stewardship, commitment to the growth of people, and building community.[18] Again, we can see how some of the main characteristics of servant leadership overlap with those of servanthood. Also, such servant leadership does not stress individualism as much as Zaragoza asserts. In fact, servant leadership actually emphasizes serving others, including building community and sharing power in decision making.

James Autry has written a book on how to practice servant leadership in building a creative team, developing great morale, and also improving bottom-line performance. Autry describes several characteristics of the leader as servant or the servant-leader, including being authentic, vulnerable, accepting, present, and useful. He also emphasizes that servant leadership involves caring for people, building a community at work, letting go of ego and being authentic, creating a workplace with meaning and good work, paying attention, and love as a basic requirement.[19] A few years ago, James Hunter wrote a best-selling story about the true essence of leadership, *The Servant*, containing timeless principles of servant leadership.[20] More recently, he has authored a book on how to become a servant leader and not a self-serving leader.[21] Similarly, Ken Blanchard and Phil Hodges have emphasized the need to "Lead like Jesus" with a servant heart in their book *The Servant Leader*.[22]

Another biblically based example of the use of the term *servant leadership* can be found in a book by Walter Wright, former president of Regent College in Vancouver, British Columbia, and now executive director of the De Pree Leadership Center in Pasadena, California. Wright presents a biblical model for influence and service, or leadership service. He states that "leadership is a relationship—a relationship in which one person seeks to influence the thoughts, behaviors, beliefs or values of another person."[23] Based on the book of Jude, Wright describes five principles of servant leadership: it is about influence and service; it is about vision and hope; it is about character and trust; it is about relationships and power; and it is about dependency and accountability.[24] He raises and provides the answers to two key questions: "Is every Christian a leader? Yes, to the extent that we seek to influence others and make a difference in the lives around us. Are we exercising servant leadership? Yes, if we have centered ourselves in the hand of God and are leading out of a relationship with God in which we know we are '*called, loved by God, and kept for Jesus Christ*,' and if we are seeking to make a difference in the world by investing ourselves in relationships with those around us that are characterized by '*mercy, peace and love*.'"[25]

Although Wright explains why he thinks every Christian is a leader who can exercise servant leadership, his definition of a leader may be too broad. While some authors such as Wright have a broad definition of leadership as a relationship of influence, others define leadership in a more specific and narrower sense. John Stott, for example, recently pointed out that "a leader . . . is someone who commands a following. To lead is to go ahead, to show the way and inspire other people to follow."[26] Based on the first four chapters of 1 Corinthians and the example of Paul, Stott draws out guidelines and lessons for Christian leadership which he also describes as servant leadership. He especially emphasizes humility. His prayer is that Christian leaders may be characterized above all else by "the meekness and gentleness of Christ" (2 Cor. 10:1).[27] There is much servanthood in the kind of Christian leadership advocated by Stott.

Bill Hybels in his recent book is even more focused and specific in his definition of leadership in the local church as Christian men and women supernaturally gifted with the spiritual gift of leadership (Rom. 12:8).[28] According to Hybels, not all Christians are called to be leaders. Christian leadership is a calling specifically to those who have the spiritual gift of leadership. In my view, such leaders still need to first be servants. Servanthood is the foundation that is absolutely necessary for proper biblical leadership to emerge in those who have been specifically called and spiritually gifted for leadership. Similarly, J. Robert Clinton has provided the following succinct description of leadership as a God-given call and gift: "Leadership is a dynamic process in which a man or woman with God-given capacity influences a specific group of God's people toward His purposes for the group."[29]

Servanthood and Leadership

In reviewing some of the voluminous literature now available on servant leadership in both secular and Christian contexts, we have seen how the term *servant leadership* has been used with different meanings. It can be a confusing term. It can also be an unbiblical concept if servanthood is used only in the service of leadership first. However, servant leadership has also been used, correctly and biblically, to refer to leadership that is founded first and foremost on servanthood: leaders with a servant's heart or attitude. Leaders who are servants first, and servants who are serving now as leaders because of a calling and gifting specifically from

God! Again, not all servants are called to be leaders. All leaders are already called to be servants first, and then leaders.

Robert Banks and Bernice Ledbetter recently provided a Christian evaluation of current leadership approaches. They emphasized the need to practice leadership through integrity, faithfulness, and service as exemplified by Jesus himself. They wrote the following wise words about servant leadership:

> Though Greenleaf insists that a leader is a servant first and only in the wake of that service is a leader, many people in authority place the main emphasis on the second word rather than on the first. . . . Ultimately they operate in ways that are not much different from those of traditional leaders. Such people have co-opted the language of servant leadership for their own agendas and purposes. Sad to say, this has often been the case in the church and in many religious organizations. Overall, the word servanthood is in danger of being viewed through the distorting lens of its contemporary misuse by those in authority. It is also in danger of being viewed too little in terms of its full Christian meaning. The trouble with the phrase "servant leadership", therefore, is that though it moves away from inadequate views of leading others, it still gets the order of the words wrong. Leadership is the key term and servant is the qualifier. What we need today are not, as is so often suggested, more *servant leaders*, but properly understood, more *leading servants*.[30]

It may therefore be more helpful to speak about *servanthood in leadership* or *the servanthood of leadership* as Max De Pree puts it, or simply *servanthood and leadership*, rather than *servant leadership*. Perhaps we should use the term *leading servants* as suggested by Banks and Ledbetter, rather than servant leaders, to refer to those servants who are called to lead as part of their service. Servant leadership can be confused with servanthood. Servanthood per se may have nothing at all to do with leadership. However, it is always the necessary foundation of all true biblical or Christian leadership, as it is of all spiritual life for those who are devoted disciples of Jesus Christ. Servanthood 101 must therefore be the foundational course in any curriculum or training program for leadership and leadership development. Leaders who are not real servants first with a servant heart are potentially dangerous. They tend to abuse power and pamper their egos. They usually end up exercising a leadership style and approach that can be destructive to themselves and their followers. This is the "dark side" of leadership. It is unlikely, however, that the term *servant leadership* will be discarded. If anything, it is being used even more widely in the leadership literature today. However, we need to be careful and more biblically-based in how we use the term *servant leadership*, especially in the context of Christian leadership.

Leadership itself is not wrong or unbiblical. It is a calling and gift (Rom. 12:8) for *some* of us who are all called to be servants first. If we are also called and gifted to be leaders, then we need to serve as leaders as best we can, empowered by the Holy Spirit. We "lead with diligence" (Rom. 12:8)! Bill Hybels has been one of the strongest advocates for such "courageous leadership," believing that "*the local church is the hope of the world and its future rests primarily in the hands of its leaders.*"[31] He issues a clarion and clear call:

> People supernaturally gifted to lead must yield themselves fully to God. They must cast powerful, biblical, God-honoring visions. They must build effective, loving, clearly focused teams. They must fire up Christ followers to give their absolute best for God. And they must insist with pit bull determination that
>
> *the gospel be preached,*
> *the lost be found,*
> *the believers be equipped,*
> *the poor be served,*
> *the lonely be enfolded into community,*
> *and God gets the credit for it all.*

> Scripture tells us exactly what will happen if leaders will do what God has called and gifted them to do. The forces of darkness will be pushed back. The Evil One, who has had his way in the world for far too long, will be forced to give ground. And the church will fulfill the redemptive purpose for which Christ called it into being.[32]

Hybels believes that the single most important aspect of leadership has to do with the art of self-leadership, which is also the toughest leadership challenge! He suggests asking several self-leadership questions regularly in order to be proficient in this crucial task of self-leadership: Is my calling sure? Is my vision clear? Is my passion hot? Am I developing fear? Are interior issues undermining my leadership? Is my peace sustainable? Is my love for God and people increasing? These are crucial questions for helping leaders overcome the "dark side" of leadership that can become toxic and destructive, and maintain their character or integrity, authenticity, wholeness, faithfulness, and servanthood, in dependence on the Holy Spirit.[33]

Leadership

The literature on leadership in general is even more substantial and overwhelming, including a growing number of books using Jesus or God and the Bible as leadership guides.[34] Rick Warren pointed out that there are thousands of books on leadership but few books on servanthood. However, those of us who are called to and gifted for leadership need to read and avail ourselves of what is good and useful in the leadership field. We need to do this always with a biblical perspective and filter with servanthood as our foundation.

For example, a well-known and widely used text on leadership by James Kouzes and Barry Posner contains some helpful material on leadership. They describe five practices and ten commitments of leadership, focusing on how leaders mobilize others to get extraordinary things done in organizations. They emphasize that credibility is the foundation of leadership. Their five practices of leadership include: model the way, inspire a shared vision, challenge the process, enable others to act, and encourage the heart.[35]

John Maxwell, a prolific writer in the area of leadership and Christian leadership, is well-known for distilling the vast leadership literature into his twenty-one irrefutable laws of leadership.[36]

In a subsequent book, *The 21 Indispensable Qualities of a Leader*, Maxwell says the following qualities will help you in becoming the person others will want to follow: "character, charisma, commitment, communication, competence, courage, discernment, focus, generosity, initiative, listening, passion, positive attitude, problem solving, relationships, responsibility, security, self-discipline, servanthood, teachability, and vision."[37] It is interesting that Maxwell includes servanthood as one of his twenty-one indispensable qualities of a leader, but he subtitles this quality as "to get ahead, put others first"! We should put others first period! He also describes the quality of servanthood as being embodied in a true servant leader who "puts others ahead of his own agenda; possesses the confidence to serve; initiates service to others; is not position-conscious; and serves out of love."[38]

Every leader has his or her own personality and preferences. Any one leadership style is therefore not adequate for the development of effective, faithful, and fruitful leadership. Hybels has emphasized the need for discovering and developing your own leadership style. In *Courageous Leadership*, he describes ten major leadership styles: visionary, directional, strategic, managing, motivational, shepherding, team-building, entrepreneurial, re-engineering, and bridge-building.[39] Hybels challenges leaders to develop their strong leadership styles and also to grow in their weaker leadership styles.

It is interesting to note that Daniel Goleman in an article entitled, "Leadership That Gets Results," in *Harvard Business Review* (March-April 2000, 78–90) reported that new research indicates that the most effective executives use a number of different leadership styles (coercive, authoritative, affiliative, democratic, pacesetting, and coaching), at the right time and in the right measure. Flexibility in leadership styles, which reflects emotional intelligence, leads to better performance and results. And it apparently can be learned. Goleman, well-known for his writings on emotional intelligence (with four fundamental capabilities: self-awareness, self-management, social awareness, and social skill), has also written a more recent book, *Primal Leadership*, with Richard Boyatzis and Annie McKee. Primal leadership focuses on realizing the power of emotional intelligence in great leadership which works through the emotions. A group or organization will flourish if its leader resonates with energy and enthusiasm. It will flounder if its leader spreads dissonance and negativity.[40]

Christian Leadership

Christian leadership that is biblical and Christ-centered will have servanthood as a crucial foundation. Christian leaders are servants of Jesus Christ specifically called and gifted by him to serve as leaders. There should be a distinct difference between Christian leadership and secular leadership. Jeffrey Greenman recently presented a preliminary sketch of the contours of "Christian Leadership." He made the following incisive statements and biblically-based conclusions regarding the distinctiveness of Christian leadership that has discipleship (and servanthood) as its very foundation:

> One of the most powerful biblical texts about the shape of Christian leadership is Mark 10:32–45. . . . Jesus teaches that the cross determines the nature of authentic leadership. Throughout the

> New Testament, leadership is cruciform—literally, "cross-shaped." . . . Leadership is defined as suffering servanthood precisely because Jesus' cross defines the meaning of service. . . . The cross-shaped pattern of Christian leadership is every bit as radical today as it was 2,000 years ago. Still today our culture gravitates toward patterns of leadership oriented by dominance, control and power. . . . When Christians become "squeezed into the world's mold" of leadership, or even deliberately adopt the world's leadership pattern, we abandon the way of the Cross and thereby compromise our distinctiveness. . . .
>
> Everything that is true of a disciple is also true of a Christian leader. The necessity of discipleship is intensified dramatically for those giving leadership to God's work in the world. Leaders are first and foremost disciples, people whose identity is found in the crucified Jesus—not in their leading, not in their ministries, not in their positions or titles or credentials, and not in their own strength. . . .
>
> Christian leaders are people who live the Cross—humbling themselves; voluntarily divesting themselves of their rights and privileges; trusting not in their own wisdom; insisting not on their own way; doing nothing out of selfish ambition; seeking not their own advantage but the benefit of others; in humility, considering others better than themselves; giving up their lives for the sake of the lost, the vulnerable, and the neglected. . . . If this is the normative pattern of leadership, it means that the crucial question for each leader is: how far are you willing to go in your discipleship?[41]

These are powerful words based on a truly biblical perspective on Christian leadership. Such leadership must be fully grounded on the foundation of discipleship that is cross-shaped or largely servanthood-shaped: it has everything to do with following Jesus all the way and living in Jesus all the way! As Eugene Peterson has put it: "Christian leadership is built on a foundation of followership—following Jesus. For those of us who are in positions of leadership—our following skills take priority over our leadership skills. Leadership that is not well-grounded in followership—following Jesus—is dangerous to both the church and the world. . . . In our Scriptures, following is far more frequently addressed than leading. The person we follow is the primary influence on the leader we become. Christians follow Jesus."[42]

Aubrey Malphurs defines Christian leaders as servants with the credibility and capacity to influence people in a particular context to pursue their God-given direction. He further describes the following core distinctives of Christian leadership that is biblically-based. A Christian leader must (1) be a Christian, (2) be a committed Christ-follower, (3) have divine revelation as his or her source of truth, (4) emphasize godly character, (5) understand the importance of motives, (6) serve through the power of the Holy Spirit, (7) practice godly servant leadership, and (8) preferably have the gift of leadership, though that's not manditory.[43]

When the Laws of Leadership and Discipleship Collide

Some of the basic principles of leadership in general, or the so-called laws of leadership, will at times collide or conflict with biblical teachings on discipleship. Laws of leadership are therefore not always irrefutable, and qualities of leadership are not always indispensable! Bill Hybels gave a stirring closing message on this topic, "When the Laws of Leadership and Discipleship Collide" at the Leadership Summit 2004 on August 14, 2004. I heard him speak via satellite at Fuller Theological Seminary.

Hybels said that while reading through the Gospel of Mark he realized that Jesus, the single most impressive leader in history, broke many of the traditional laws of leadership. He provided several examples of this in Mark. For instance, in Mark 1:35, Jesus broke the law of momentum when he walked away from the crowds and spent time instead in solitude and prayer. In Mark 10, he broke the law of leveraging your time and influence wisely (by influencing key people and not wasting time) by severely rebuking the disciples for trying to send the children away. And, as one more example, in Mark 14:34 Jesus showed deep vulnerability and "weakness" in his anguish in the Garden of Gethsemane, and therefore broke the law of being strong for the team!

Hybels himself has had to learn to break some of the traditional laws of leadership in his ministry over the past thirty years. For example, when Willow Creek Community Church was growing by the hundreds each week, he decided to derail the momentum train by following God's leading to preach on 100 percent discipleship. The church lost a few members as a result. Another example Hybels gave was when the Holy Spirit prompted him to go to an event for mentally and physically challenged people in his church. As a leader and senior pastor, he was supposed to follow the leadership law of leveraging his time and influence on key people. He struggled with this one and shared that God had to speak to him along these lines: "It shouldn't be this hard, Bill—what's happening to you? You better slow your pace down and sort out all of this when the laws of leadership collide with the laws and demands of discipleship."

Although Hybels still believes that leaders should read and learn all they can about great leadership, he is now convinced that occasionally the laws of leadership and the laws of discipleship will collide and be in conflict. He emphatically challenges us at such times to *always* decide on the side of discipleship! He reminds us that the traditional laws of leadership are not infallible or inerrant: only the Bible, God's Word, is inspired and 100 percent infallible or inerrant. He acknowledged that the more he leads, the more dependent he has learned to be on the Holy Spirit in every area of his life. He asserted that the power of the Holy Spirit is the leader's best friend. Hybels concluded that the Holy Spirit is crucial in leadership and discipleship. I fully agree with Hybels. The Holy Spirit is truly "indispensable and irrefutable" in leadership and discipleship and life itself! In fact, I believe that the laws of leadership will collide with the laws and demands of discipleship more often than we would like. We need the presence and power of the Holy Spirit, in deep friendship with Jesus our best friend, to always choose the way of discipleship, the way of servanthood: Following and living in Jesus all the way! This is ultimately also the way and path of biblical Christian leadership. It is distinctively different from secular leadership that often stresses CEO and MBA leadership models and needs to be carefully and biblically critiqued and filtered.

Interestingly enough in *Geeks and Geezers*, leadership experts Warren Bennis and Robert Thomas wrote about how era, values, and defining moments shape leaders (geeks referring to our youngest leaders, and geezers to our oldest leaders). They present a new model of who is likely to become a leader and remain a leader, focusing especially on the "crucibles of leadership": crucial transformational experiences, including failure and suffering, that result in a leader either being totally devastated and broken, or empowered to learn and to lead. True leaders, young or old, have an amazing capacity to embrace and grow from their crucibles. They also have other crucial qualities such as adaptive capacity, the ability to engage others through shared meaning, voice, integrity (character), and a youthful curiosity or zest for knowledge called "neoteny."[44] One of the crucibles that Christian leaders need to embrace and grow from is when laws of leadership and discipleship clash. In such situations of struggle, as Hybels has so eloquently shared, Christian leaders painfully learn to depend more fully on the Holy Spirit and break the so-called laws of leadership when necessary. In doing so they will paradoxically become better Christian leaders: more fruitful and faithful disciples and servants of Jesus Christ.

6

True Service Versus Self-Righteous Service

Servanthood, servant leadership, leadership, Christian leadership. We have just seen, in the previous chapter, how these terms can be confusing. We therefore need to use them carefully and clearly. In this chapter we return to servanthood: being plain servants and not necessarily servant leaders. True servanthood in Christ leads to true service, versus self-righteous service that is more characteristic of servitude or ego-centered activity. Before I go on to describe several significant differences between true service and self-righteous service, following Richard Foster,[1] we need to have a deeper understanding and picture of what servanthood really looks like.

Being Bondslaves of Jesus Christ

In several passages of Scripture, the Greek word *doulos* is now usually translated as *servant* but more literally means *bondservant* or *slave*. In Philippians 2:7, Jesus "made himself nothing, taking the very nature of a servant" (*doulos* or slave) who was fully submissive to the Father's will (e.g., John 4:34; 5:30; 6:38). Similarly Peter (2 Peter 1:1), Paul (Rom. 1:1; Phil. 1:1; Titus 1:1), James (James 1:1), and Jude (Jude 1) in the New Testament refer to themselves as a *doulos*—a bondservant or slave of Jesus Christ. They gladly and willingly identified themselves as such because they had surrendered themselves fully to the Lordship of Christ. Jesus was their Master or Lord and Savior, and they submitted to his leading and control.

As Nancy Leigh DeMoss has pointed out, Exodus 21:1–2, 5–6 provides a description of a Hebrew servant or slave for life, someone who chooses not to go free in the seventh year of slavery or servanthood, for love of the master. The servant's or slave's ear was pierced with an awl, and that hole in the ear stood as a mark of servanthood for life, a bondslave.[2] DeMoss shares that choosing to be a bondslave of Jesus Christ is the greatest calling anyone can have from God: "I have come to believe that there is no greater calling than to be marked as His slave—to choose to give my life in the service of the Master I have grown to know and love and trust. For many years, my prayer has been, 'Oh, God, make me a woman with a hole in my ear; I want to be identified as a slave of Jesus Christ.'"[3]

DeMoss shares two other contemporary stories of people who likewise chose to be Jesus' bondslaves or servants for life. Josef Tson, a Romanian pastor and Christian leader, was exiled from his native country in 1981. He suffered great and lengthy persecution before coming to the United States where he stayed and ministered for about ten years before returning to Romania to continue to serve the Lord there. DeMoss met him and his wife, Elizabeth, in the early 1980s at a meeting of Christian workers where he was a speaker. When asked how he should be introduced, Josef chose to be described simply as "a slave of Jesus Christ," although he was an articulate, Oxford-educated theologian![4]

Similarly, a young couple named Bill and Vonette Bright, on a Sunday afternoon in the spring of 1951, said the following prayer together in their living room, under deep conviction: "Lord, we surrender our lives irrevocably to You and to do Your will. We want to love and serve You with all of our hearts for the rest of our lives."

DeMoss further notes: "Bill describes one further step they took that day as an expression of their heart's intent: 'We actually wrote and signed a contract committing our whole lives to Him, relinquishing all of our rights, all of our possessions, everything we would ever own, giving to Him, our dear Lord and Master, everything. In the words of the Apostle Paul, [my wife] and I became that Sunday afternoon voluntary slaves of Jesus.'"[5] Bill and Vonette Bright then founded and led one of the largest Christian organizations to date: Campus Crusade for Christ. When Bill Bright was diagnosed with a terminal lung disease which eventually took his life, he expressed his desire and Vonette's as well, to have as the only epitaph on their tombstone: "Slave of Jesus Christ."

Two years before the Lord took him home in July 2003, Bill Bright shared the following ten keys to anointed leadership or ministry for the Lord: "I've had fifty-five years of walking with the Lord—most of them since my student days at Fuller. If I had only ten things to share with the Fuller faculty, alumni/ae, and students, it would be these ten keys to having an anointed ministry for our Lord:

1. Discover the character of God.
2. Surrender to the Lordship of Christ.
3. Be filled with the Holy Spirit.
4. Study the Word of God.
5. Practice spiritual multiplication.
6. Make prayer and fasting part of your program.
7. Ask God to give you a vision.

8. Keep your priorities straight.
9. Work as unto the Lord.
10. Have faith—trust God!"[6]

These ten keys are also keys to anointed servanthood, for Bill Bright was truly a servant or bondslave of Jesus Christ!

Hope of the Church

Bill Hybels is well-known for his strong conviction that the local church is the hope of the world and its future rests primarily in the hands of its leaders. I believe instead that servants (including servants who are called to be leaders) are the hope of the church. More recently, Hybels clarified his view in a book, *The Volunteer Revolution*, on unleashing the power of all Christians: "I believe that the church is the hope of the world. But that hope rests on the willingness of volunteers from all walks of life—doctors, teachers, at-home moms, business executives, college students, nurses, grandmothers, retired engineers, carpenters, dentists, hairdressers, high school kids, grocery-store clerks—to be mobilized, empowered, and used by God."[7] He shared how a lack of funding in the early history of his church forced him and his co-workers to learn a profound truth: "The church was designed to be primarily a volunteer organization. The power of the church truly is the power of everybody as men and women, young, and old, offer their gifts to work out God's redemptive plan."[8] Servants, or bondslaves of Jesus Christ, whether volunteers or paid church staff, are the real hope of the church. And servanthood is the secret to the most fulfilling and meaningful life we can ever experience. In describing servanthood as "the great gamble" in life, Hybels concluded: ". . . accept the fundamental paradox of the Christian life: that following Jesus into radical servanthood is the sure pathway to fullness of life. Sooner or later, everybody has to decide where to place their bets on life's great gamble. Where have you placed yours? On a self-centered lifestyle? Or on Jesus' model of servanthood? Where has it taken you? If you're not pleased with your answer, grab a serving towel. It'll be worth the gamble."[9] Ultimately, choosing to follow Jesus all the way in radical servanthood is not really a gamble or risk at all. It is actually the wisest and surest way of experiencing the deepest fulfillment of which human beings are capable. We all have a God-shaped vacuum that only God can fill in Christ, as we follow him in radical discipleship and servanthood. Such servanthood will lead to true service rather than self-righteous service that comes out of servitude and ego-centeredness.

True Service Versus Self-Righteous Service

Richard Foster, in *Celebration of Discipline*, describes nine characteristics of true service that flows out of a servant's heart in radical servanthood versus nine characteristics of self-righteous service that is more ego-centered.[10] *True service* has the following features: (1) It comes from a relationship with the divine Other deep inside (i.e., deep friendship with Jesus); (2) It finds it impossible to distinguish the small from the large service; (3) It rests centered in holiness; (4) It is free of the need to calculate results; (5) It is indiscriminate in its ministry (i.e., it serves one and all equally); (6) It ministers simply and faithfully because there is a need (i.e., regardless of feelings); (7) It is a lifestyle (i.e., servanthood for life in all of life); (8) It can withhold the service as freely as perform it; and (9) It builds community.

Self-righteous service on the other hand has the following characteristics: (1) It comes through human effort (i.e., usually with much planning and programming and little or no prayer); (2) It is impressed with the "big deal" (because it is ultimately self-centered or ego-focused); (3) It requires external rewards; (4) It is highly concerned with results (and statistics!); (5) It picks and chooses whom to serve; (6) It is affected by moods and whims (i.e., feelings rule the service rather than service rules the feelings); (7) It is temporary; (8) It is insensitive; and (9) It fractures community. Ultimately, self-righteous service centers in the glorification of the individual.

True servanthood characterized by true service involves choosing to be a servant or bondslave of Jesus Christ. It is not simply choosing to serve. This difference is crucial. Foster wisely points out: "Right here we must see the difference between choosing to serve and choosing to be a servant. When we choose to serve, we are still in charge. We decide whom we will serve and when we will serve. And if we are in charge, we will worry a great deal about anyone stepping on us, that is, taking charge over us. But when we choose to be a servant, we give up the right to be in charge. There is great freedom in this. If we voluntarily choose to be a servant, we surrender the right to decide who and when we will serve. We become available and vulnerable."[11] Foster also notes that true service, especially when done in hiddenness (secrecy or anonymity), is most conducive to the development of humility. We will cover servanthood and humility in more detail in a later chapter of this book.

True service by real servants who are bondslaves of Jesus Christ can be shown in many and various ways. Foster lists several of them, including the service of hiddenness (doing a service in secret or keeping it private and unknown), the service of small things, the service of guarding the reputation of others, the service of being served, the service of common courtesy, the service of hospitality, the service of listening, the service of bearing the burdens of each other, and the service of sharing the Word of life with one another.[12] Another crucial area of true service is the service of praying for others, which may be the most loving and important thing we can do for one another. Ajith Fernando, in his powerful book *Jesus Driven Ministry*, emphasizes prayer as central and essential in ministry to others: "I have come to believe that praying for those I lead is the most important thing that I do as a leader. This belief is based on what the Bible says about the power of prayer. . . . If prayer is the most important thing that we do, then we should work at developing our prayer life."[13] Fernando goes on to write: "One cannot take shortcuts in the life of prayer. All Christian ministry is ministry in the Spirit, and for that we must linger with the Spirit. We simply cannot have a ministry that has spiritual depth, and therefore lasting effects, unless our lives are steeped in prayer."[14]

True service, according to Foster, comes first from a relationship with the divine Other deep inside, or a deep friendship with Jesus as we serve him. Affirmed and fully accepted by God in such a loving relationship with him, real servants have a deep sense of identity, security, and significance. Fernando asserts that true servanthood results from such acceptance by God, but serving without this sense of God's acceptance can be dangerous because it can lead to behaviors similar to self-righteous service.[15] It is therefore essential for servants or bondslaves of Jesus Christ to grow deep in God, integrating sound theology and prayer as Edmund Chan has described in his helpful book.[16]

As I write this chapter, several examples of true service done by real servants come to mind. I think of a church member, a senior executive of a bank, who has faithfully served in various capacities in our church over many years. He has served on a number of church boards and committees and has cooked on Sundays as part of a rotating team that serves lunch for several hundred people after the worship services. And he has swept and mopped the kitchen floors many times. I have wept inside and sometimes outwardly as I have quietly seen his Christlike, loving, humble servanthood in action.

I think of a pastor in Malaysia, on a recent speaking/preaching trip I made there, who insisted on carrying my briefcase everywhere he drove me and asked about my local favorite foods so he could obtain them for me to enjoy. He did all this in an unassuming manner, without drawing attention to himself. I had to firmly say "No" to some of the things he so kindly offered to do for me. I also think of a friend in Canada who recently became the senior pastor of a church. He felt inadequate to fill such a position and was utterly surprised when he was first approached to do so. Yet, out of loving obedience to Jesus, he accepted the call. He is serving faithfully and humbly, spending much time in prayer daily for his church and city. He even called to let me know he was praying for me and the writing of this book. His ministry in prayer and intercession reminds me of what I believe Billy Graham has often referred to as the real heroes or heroines behind his worldwide and amazingly fruitful evangelistic ministry: the unknown numbers of people who pray and intercede for him, sometimes for hours, every day. I think especially of the example of an elderly woman, bedridden with a stroke for years yet faithfully praying daily for Billy Graham and his evangelistic ministry. I also remember and am deeply thankful for the dozens of people in my church who pray daily for me and my ministry, providing the prayer covering or prayer shield I need as I serve the Lord Jesus. They are real servants lovingly and faithfully involved in the true service of intercessory prayer for others.

I can think of many other examples, such as all the volunteers in my church and in other churches who serve faithfully in so many ways, week after week, month after month, year after year. As Hybels has put it, a volunteer revolution is happening in churches all over the world! Servants or bondslaves of Jesus Christ, engaged in true service, are truly the hope of the church.

The SHAPE of True Service

Rick Warren, in *The Purpose-Driven Life*,[17] answered the question of "What on earth am I here for?" by emphasizing that it's not about you: it's about God first! He then describes the five major purposes of our lives, according to God and his Word, the Bible. They are

1. You were planned for God's pleasure.
2. You were formed for God's family.
3. You were created to become like Christ.
4. You were shaped for serving God.
5. You were made for a mission.

These five purposes revolve around worship, fellowship, discipleship, ministry, and evangelism. They are also the basic purposes of the church, and Warren has described them in an earlier book, *The Purpose-Driven Church*.[18]

In writing about the purpose of ministry, Warren emphasized that we are all shaped for serving God, each one of us with our particular SHAPE: "Whenever God gives us an assignment, he always equips us with what we need to accomplish it. This custom combination of capabilities is called your SHAPE:

Spiritual Gifts
Heart
Abilities
Personality
Experience."[19]

It is important for us to discover how the Lord has formed us in our unique SHAPE for true service that is particular to us. Warren's book[20] as well as Peter Wagner's *Your Spiritual Gifts Can Help Your Church Grow*[21] are especially helpful to servants wanting to unwrap their spiritual gifts and discover their specific SHAPE for true service.

With regard to the experience component of SHAPE, Warren lists at least six kinds of experiences from our past that we should learn from and use in our service: *family*, *educational*, *vocational*, *spiritual*, *ministry*, and *painful* experiences. He emphasizes: "It is this last category, *painful* experiences, that God uses the most to prepare you for ministry. *God never wastes a hurt*! In fact, your *greatest* ministry will most likely come out of your greatest hurt."[22] We will deal with servanthood and suffering in more detail in the next chapter.

7

Servanthood and Suffering

It is a basic fact of life that we all experience suffering in some form or other during our lives on earth. This is true for all human beings, not just for Christians or servants of Christ. Jesus tells us clearly: "In this world you will have trouble. But take heart! I have overcome the world" (John 16:33). Jesus himself can be described not only as the Master Servant (as we have seen in chapter 2), but also as the Suffering Servant (see Isa. 52:13–53:12) who is "familiar with suffering" (Isa. 53:3). As servants or bondslaves of Jesus, we too will experience suffering and sacrifice in our lives as we follow him. He has called us as his disciples and servants to deny ourselves, take up our cross daily, and follow him (Luke 9:23), even to death if necessary (John 15:12–13; Phil. 2:5–11). Like the apostle Paul, our response as Christ's servants should be: "I want to know Christ and the power of his resurrection and the fellowship of sharing in his sufferings, becoming like him in his death" (Phil. 3:10). The way of servanthood and discipleship is cross-shaped: it is the way of the cross. It is not easy; it is difficult and painful. The church in the West often preaches a gospel of success, satisfaction, and self-esteem. Jesus instead speaks to us about suffering and sacrifice that ultimately lead to deep joy from him and in him (John 15:11). If we surrender and yield to him, depending on his grace in our suffering, we will grow to become more like him. And we will experience the deepest joy possible!

Suffering: Becoming More Like Jesus

Rick Warren reminds us that "we learn things about God in suffering that we can't learn any other way." He quotes Joni Eareckson Tada who notes: "When life is rosy, we may slide by with knowing about Jesus, with imitating him and quoting him and speaking of him. But only in suffering will we *know* Jesus."[1] Warren especially wants to encourage us with the truth of Romans 8:28, which is a promise to those who are God's children in Christ: "And we know that in all things God works for the good of those who love him, who have been called according to his purpose." His purpose in Romans 8:29 is "that God's children be conformed to the likeness of his Son."[2]

As real servants of Christ, we will therefore embrace suffering and sacrifice when and where necessary, without glorifying suffering. We can be reassured and encouraged by 1 Peter 4:12–13: "Dear friends, do not be surprised at the painful trial you are suffering, as though something strange were happening to you. But rejoice that you participate in the sufferings of Christ, so that you may be overjoyed when his glory is revealed." And 1 Peter 5:10: "And the God of all grace, who called you to his eternal glory in Christ, after you have suffered a little while, will himself restore you and make you strong, firm, and steadfast." We can also be confident of God's good purposes in our suffering and sacrifice as his servants, trusting and rejoicing in him for molding and making us more Christlike. We can take comfort in God's Word, the Bible, when it says in James 1:2–4: "Consider it pure joy, my brothers, whenever you face trials of many kinds, because you know that the testing of your faith develops perseverance. Perseverance must finish its work so that you may be mature and complete, not lacking anything." And in Romans 5:3–5: "Not only so, but we also rejoice in our sufferings, because we know that suffering produces perseverance; perseverance, character; and character, hope. And hope does not disappoint us, because God has poured out his love into our hearts by the Holy Spirit, whom he has given us."

God is lovingly and deeply working in us through our suffering and sacrifice to mature us into more Christlike character. He is making us into more compassionate and loving servants who love God with everything we are and have and who love others deeply (Mark 12:28–31). Suffering is essential for producing deeper love in our lives, the kind of agape love that Jesus commands us to have for each other (John 13:34–35; 15:12–13, 17). In fact, we will learn the truth of what Kathleen Santucci wrote in a letter some years ago: "One must suffer to learn to love. . . . One must suffer to learn to know God and be a partner with Him in this world. . . . Suffering helps to purge one's life of sin."[3]

Paul Billheimer wrote: "There is simply no way to explain the Biblical teaching on the glory of suffering and tribulation, except as an apprenticeship for the throne. No love without suffering. No rulership without love. Therefore, only if we suffer shall we reign with him. . . . Remember, you are destined for the throne! God is training you now. Your trials are not an accident: no suffering is purposeless. Your eternal profit is in view. Therefore, don't waste your sorrows! . . . LIFE IS FOR LEARNING AGAPE LOVE."[4]

What is most comforting and life-transforming for us in our suffering as servants is that the Lord is *with* us in our suffering: He weeps and bleeds with us and for us. He is touched by our pain and is able to sympathize with our weaknesses (Heb. 4:15).

God's Purposes in Our Suffering

Joni Eareckson Tada, who has lived in a wheelchair for more than thirty years, and Steven Estes have written a book *When God Weeps: Why Our Sufferings Matter to the Almighty*. Based on Scripture, they list thirty-six benefits or blessings from God's hand in hardship and suffering. The following are some examples:

- God uses suffering to refine, perfect, strengthen, and keep us from falling (Ps. 66:8–9; Heb. 2:10).
- Suffering allows the life of Christ to be manifested in our mortal flesh (2 Cor. 4:7–11).
- Suffering bankrupts us, making us dependent on God (2 Cor. 12:9).
- Suffering teaches us humility (2 Cor. 12:7).
- Suffering teaches us that God is more concerned with character than comfort (Rom. 5:3–4; Heb. 12:10–11).
- Suffering teaches us that the greatest good of the Christian life is not absence of pain but Christlikeness (Rom 8:28–29; 2 Cor. 4:8–10).
- Suffering can be a chastisement from God for sin and rebellion (Ps. 107:17).
- Obedience and self-control are learned from suffering (Ps. 119:67; Rom. 5:1–5; Heb. 5:8).
- Suffering strengthens and allows us to comfort others who are weak (2 Cor. 1:3–11).[5]

These are great and precious promises or truths from Scripture that can help us better endure and even embrace times of suffering. God will ultimately bring good out of our suffering. He will make us better servants, who are more faithful and fruitful (John 15:1–5). He will also comfort us in our troubles and suffering, so that we can comfort others in their suffering with the comfort we ourselves have received from God (2 Cor. 1:3–4).

Suffering and Shattered Dreams

Suffering is still painful, sometimes excruciatingly painful, despite all of the verses we have memorized and believe about the good purposes God has in our suffering. Suffering may be particularly overwhelming and devastating when we experience shattered dreams. In his deeply helpful book, Larry Crabb describes shattered dreams as God's unexpected pathway to joy. Based on the story of Naomi in the book of Ruth, Crabb presents three basic ideas related to tasting and seeing that the Lord is good even when the bottom falls out of our lives:

> 1. *God wants to bless you.* . . . 2. *The deepest pleasure we're capable of experiencing is a direct encounter with God.* . . . But we almost always mistake lesser pleasures for this greatest pleasure and live our lives chasing them. We're not in touch with our appetite for God. 3. So the Holy Spirit awakens that appetite. *He uses the pain of shattered dreams to help us discover our desire for God*, to help us begin dreaming the highest dream. . . . *Our shattered dreams are never random. They are always a piece in a larger puzzle, a chapter in a larger story*. Pain is a tragedy. But it's never only a tragedy. For the Christian, it's always a necessary mile on the long journey to joy.[6]

Crabb also draws out three essential lessons of brokenness from the book of Ruth:

> Lesson 1—*The good news of the gospel is not that God will provide a way to make life easier. . . . He will make our lives better. We will be empowered to draw close to God and to love others well . . . to glorify God.* Lesson 2—*When God seems most absent from us, He is doing*

> *His most important work in us.* Lesson 3—*Bad times provide an opportunity to know God that blessings can never provide.*[7]

These precious lessons on shattered dreams and suffering as God's unexpected pathway to deep joy are crucial lessons for servants of Jesus to learn. Such experiences of shattered dreams are not strange to those who have walked deeply with God. Years ago, A. W. Tozer wrote about a similar process, which he called "the ministry of the night":

> To do His supreme work of grace within you, He will take away from your heart everything you love most. Everything you trust in will go from you. Piles of ashes will lie where your most precious treasures used to be . . . slowly you will discover God's love in your suffering. . . . You will feel and understand *the ministry of the night*; its power to purify, to detach, to humble, to destroy the fear of death, and what is more important to you at the moment, the fear of life. And you will learn that sometimes pain can do what even joy cannot, such as exposing the vanity of earth's trifles and filling your heart with longing for the peace of heaven.[8]

The Dark Night of the Soul

What is the difference between shattered dreams, or the ministry of the night, and what St. John of the Cross described as "the dark night of the soul"? There are some similarities between the ministry of the night and the dark night of the soul, but they are not identical experiences. The dark night of the soul (see Isa. 50:10) is a more comprehensive concept. It has become a popular term used somewhat superficially and sometimes erroneously by people today who are interested in or curious about spirituality. Richard Foster has pointed out that the "dark night" is not a destructive, punitive, or bad thing, but instead it is meant to draw us closer to God and to set us free. It may involve experiencing dryness, aloneness, or even lostness, removing any overdependence on the emotional life.[9]

Gerald May recently pointed out that the dark night of the soul is often wrongly used in circles of pop spirituality to refer to misfortunes of all kinds, ranging from major tragedies to minor disappointments. He clarifies the more accurate meaning of the dark night of the soul: "It can happen to anyone. I believe that in some way it happens to everyone. Yet it is much more than simple misfortune. It is a deep transformation, a movement toward indescribable freedom and joy. And in truth it doesn't always have to be unpleasant! . . . The dark night is a profoundly good thing. It is an ongoing spiritual process in which we are liberated from attachments and compulsions and empowered to live and love more freely. Sometimes this letting go of old ways is painful, occasionally even devastating. But this is not why the night is called 'dark.' The darkness of the night implies nothing sinister, only that the liberation takes place in hidden ways, beneath our knowledge, and understanding. More than anything, I think the dark night of the soul gives *meaning* to life. . . . The meaning revealed in the dark night is beyond understanding . . . it is about nothing other than love: love for God, love for one another, love for creation, love for life itself."[10]

The dark night of the soul does not necessarily mean devastatingly painful experiences or shattered dreams. It doesn't always have to be unpleasant, but it can be. It can also be not just unpleasant but painful. It is therefore a more comprehensive concept than the ministry of the night. Whatever shape or form the dark night of the soul takes, however, it leads ultimately to greater freedom by diminishing attachment, to love for God and other people in a totally unfettered way, and to deeper union with God such that our desire is now the same as God's desire.[11] This is a crucial process for us as servants of Jesus to undergo and embrace so that we end up wanting what he wants and doing only his will. This is what true service with a servant's heart is all about!

Suffering and Brokenness

A common element present in the experiences and processes described so far, whether it is the ministry of the night or shattered dreams, or the dark night of the soul, is that of brokenness. We read the words of David in Psalm 51:16–17: "You do not delight in sacrifice, or I would bring it; you do not take pleasure in burnt offerings. The sacrifices of God are a broken spirit; a broken and contrite heart, O God, you will not despise." Brokenness is essential for us and precious to God.

Alan Nelson noted that brokenness can be defined as "reduced to submission, tamed," and therefore applies to the taming of the soul.[12] The goal of brokenness is to deny oneself, becoming less, so that Christ can become more in us (John 3:27–30), realizing that we can do nothing apart from Christ (John 15:5).[13] Nelson also points out that brokenness is close to other concepts such as "heart allegiance," "pruning," "crucified living," and "total surrender" when we come to the end of ourselves and utterly depend on God.[14] While brokenness often involves experiences of suffering, it is not the same as suffering. Whatever tames our souls and helps us to surrender to God, even if it involves little or no suffering, is an experience of brokenness.

Nelson provides a helpful differentiation between *voluntary and involuntary brokenness*. He describes involuntary brokenness as "that which pops up when we least expect it. It appears in the form of health issues, financial distress, relationship turmoil, job disruption, dream frustrations, aging milestones, and periods of spiritual and emotional dryness. What makes such times difficult is that we discover our finiteness and our need to turn over new parts of our lives to the Lord. . . . Many events come our way, involuntarily, which can serve as lessons in brokenness. . . . These regular bumps and bruises can tenderize us if our attitudes are right. If we respond poorly, we are likely to become critical, cynical, and stressed out. Becoming tender is the way of faith."[15]

He describes voluntary brokenness as "the intentional exercise of submitting yourself to God. It is initiating the attitude of surrender as a continuance of prior breaking and can also prevent the need for future breaking. Much of this activity revolves around the spiritual disciplines . . . the behaviors of brokenness."[16]

Voluntary brokenness, then, can be maintained by the regular practice of the spiritual disciplines that enable us to submit and surrender to God. Nelson, following Richard Foster and Dallas Willard, goes on to briefly describe the following spiritual disciplines as behaviors of brokenness. *Behaviors of Abstinence*: solitude, silence, fasting, simplicity, chastity, sacrifice, and secrecy. *Disciplines of Activity*: study, prolonged prayer, celebration, service, fellowship, confession, and submission.[17]

While the traditional spiritual disciplines can help us maintain voluntary brokenness, they are not without their dangers. If spiritual disciplines are practiced legalistically, they can harm rather than help our spiritual life and growth in Christ by fostering self-righteousness, self-sufficiency, arrogance, and the like. Gary Thomas therefore points out that this is why the *authentic disciplines* are such a vital addition to the traditional spiritual disciplines: "They turn us away from human effort—from men and women seeking the face of God—and turn us back toward God seeking the face of men and women."[18]

The authentic disciplines (i.e., the disciplines of selflessness, waiting, suffering, persecution, social mercy, forgiveness, mourning, contentment, sacrifice, hope, and fear) are mostly initiated outside of us: "God brings them into our life when he wills and as he wills. . . . This is a God-ordained spirituality, dependent on his sovereignty. . . . There's no pride left when God takes me through a time of suffering. There's no self-righteousness when I am called to wait. There is no religiosity when I am truly mourning. This is a spirituality I can't control, I can't initiate, I can't bring about. It is a radical dependence on God's husbandry. All I can do is try to appreciate it and learn from it."[19] The greater end of going through these authentic disciplines initiated or sent by God is "*learning to love with God's love* and *learning to serve with God's power.*"[20]

God's power and love are essential in servanthood, especially in reaching out to the world with the gospel of Jesus Christ. As servants of Christ, we will weep and bleed for the lost as we walk deeply and daily with the Suffering Servant who bled and died and rose again for us. We will help our churches to be more of an "Antioch church."[21] An Antioch church is so concerned for the lost that its priorities are directed by the mandate of the Great Commission (Matt. 28:18–20) to go to the ends of the earth to make disciples of all nations, as his witnesses empowered by the Holy Spirit (Acts 1:8). We need to overcome the tendency of many churches today to remain a "Jerusalem church" that is so wrapped up in its own programs and misplaced, self-centered priorities that it is ineffective in spreading the gospel to the ends of the earth. To help our churches become Antioch churches, we need the anointing and empowering of the Holy Spirit (Acts 1:8). In this regard, Ross Paterson emphasizes the need for brokenness, humility, and utter dependency on God for such power and anointing from the Holy Spirit to be released.[22]

I recently challenged the church members at First Evangelical Church Glendale, where I serve as senior pastor, to become an Antioch church: broken and yet filled with the Spirit's power and anointing to serve our best friend Jesus in faithful and fruitful ways to the ends of the earth. Several years ago, I similarly challenged a group of pastors and church leaders at a spiritual retreat held near Jakarta, Indonesia, to surrender their lives fully to the Lord Jesus, to servanthood even unto death. All one hundred and forty of them stood up in response—and wept. My Indonesian translator and I also broke down and wept. We all experienced a deeper brokenness and a special anointing of the presence and power of the Holy Spirit. As we wept, we felt the compassionate heart of Jesus for the people of Indonesia. The Indonesian pastors and church leaders knew that rededicating themselves to servanthood could literally mean death. Some of these leaders were from parts of the country where Christians had recently been martyred for their faith and churches had been burned to the ground. This was a very moving and touching experience for me. I realized afresh that suffering as a servant of Jesus can sometimes mean death for his sake.

While martyrdom, or literally dying for Jesus, may be God's will for some of us, it is his will for all disciples and servants of Jesus to die daily to our selfish ambitions and sinful, false self. Erwin McManus, challenging us to be daring enough to become the church God had in mind, wrote: "The New Testament word for 'witness' is the same as for 'martyr'. We have come to know martyrs as those who have died for their faith. The purpose of church cannot be to survive or even to thrive but to serve. And sometimes servants die in the serving. . . . Following Jesus is a dangerous undertaking. He was willing to die on our behalf. The only way that I could truly follow God was to die to myself and live for him. Only dead men [and women] can follow the God of the Cross."[23]

Examples of Suffering Servanthood

There are many biblical characters who are examples of suffering servants of God, including Job and the apostle Paul. I will not provide a review of them, many of whom are listed in Hebrews 11. Instead, I want to share about the suffering of a contemporary theologian, author, and educator who has written several powerful and deeply spiritual and theological books. Her name is Marva Dawn. I have been deeply touched and greatly blessed by her testimony and writings. In one of her recent books, she emphasizes the need for us to come to the end of our own powers and in our weakness to depend fully on God and his tabernacling, or dwelling with us. She openly and vulnerably shares about her own suffering and weaknesses as she serves the Lord she loves so much:

> Some days I'm thoroughly exhausted from all the strain of trying to manage with arthritic hands, a crippled leg, a blind eye, a deaf ear, kidneys functioning around 17 percent, dead intestinal and stomach nerves resulting in no peristalsis, pain leftover from cancer and jaw surgeries, the imminent possibility of losing vision in my remaining eye, and now the possibility that the bone dropping from the fusion of my foot will continue generating sores that will eventually necessitate amputation. And that isn't the whole list. Does God really need me to be this weak?
>
> Yes!
>
> I believe that, although I don't understand it. Part of our human weakness is to recognize that the workings of God are "hidden", mysterious beyond our human comprehension. In the midst of our unknowing, however, God comes afresh with new tabernacling.[24]

Dawn translates the well-known words of the apostle Paul, from 2 Corinthians 11:30 and 12:7–10, who also suffered greatly in his servanthood and Christian leadership, emphasizing that the goal is for our power to come to its end, thus: "If it is necessary to continue boasting, I will boast of those things which show my weakness . . . therefore, to keep me from being too elated, a thorn in the flesh was given to me, a messenger of Satan to knock me about, to keep me from being too elated. Three times I appealed to the Lord concerning this, that it might depart from me, but he said to me, 'My grace is sufficient for you, for [your] power is brought to its end in weakness.' All the more gladly, then, will I boast in my weaknesses that the power of Christ [not mine!] may tabernacle upon me. Therefore, I take delight in weaknesses, in insults, in necessities, in persecutions and calamities for the sake of Christ, for when I am weak, then I am strong."[25] In a similar vein, in his exposition of Second Corinthians, Roy Clements states the following about Paul the apostle: "He teaches us as much by his example as by his words what it really means to stay there at the foot of the cross. For only there can we learn the most vital and yet the most paradoxical lesson of all—*the strength of weakness*."[26] And J. I. Packer writes: "May God in his great mercy weaken us all!"[27]

Ajith Fernando however reminds us: "Suffering is not easy. Those who make love their goal in life are going to hurt deeply when they are rejected, unappreciated, exploited, or opposed by the very people they seek to love. But that is the lot of God's servants. However, as we face the prospect of suffering, God will remind us that, just as Christ's sufferings produced great glory, our sufferings will also bring great glory to God."[28] He then gives several examples of God's servants—William Carey, Helen Roseveare, George Mueller, and John Wesley—who suffered situations of extreme crisis but continued serving God, depending on his provision and sufficient grace. Severe frustrations, disappointments, and persecutions have often been experienced by those trying to reach out to the lost. Yet churches have grown despite, and perhaps even because of, such difficulties and sufferings.[29] Similarly, Thomas points out that maturity in the faith may actually mean more suffering and not less. He notes the following examples of so-called spiritual giants who wrote Christian classics, and how they had bitterly difficult lives: "Augustine died of a wasting disease . . . Teresa of Avila suffered through years of intense migraines; Brother Lawrence never got over his chronic gout; Martin Luther died a difficult death following a long string of illnesses; the great Puritan writer Richard Baxter wrote one of his most famous works while a grotesquely large tumor protruded out of his body; Francis of Assisi . . . was nearly blind as he wrote."[30] Thomas calls the fire-testing seasons of our lives from a loving Father "severe gifts,"[31] or what I have often referred to as God's "severe mercies."

One final set of examples of suffering servanthood has to do with those who died for their faith. According to dc Talk in *Jesus*

Freaks, Volume II, the total number of Christian martyrs who have died for their faith since the time of Jesus, from AD 33–2000, is 69,421,230![32] Over 69 million martyrs. In this context of persecution and martyrdom, John Stott wrote, "Tertullian, addressing the rulers of the Roman Empire, cried out: 'Kill us, torture us, condemn us, grind us to dust. . . . The more you mow us down, the more we grow; the seed is the blood of Christians.' . . . Persecution will refine the church, but not destroy it. If it leads to prayer and praise, to an acknowledgement of the sovereignty of God and of solidarity with Christ in his sufferings, then—however painful—it may even be welcome."[33]

Servanthood and suffering can therefore include persecution and even death or martyrdom. As servants of Jesus, we can embrace suffering, including brokenness, voluntary and involuntary. Suffering is part of the way of the cross. It also leads to the power of his resurrection and the greater glory of God! And it can produce deep humility. Out of such "crucibles" of suffering we can become better servants and better Christian leaders if we are also called to leadership. We can become better people in and through our suffering, if we yield to the Lord, depend on his grace, and let him work out his deep and good purposes. Ultimately, suffering can help us as servants of Christ to worship God more deeply and fully with even greater satisfaction in him, thereby enabling us to glorify him even more! Suffering and worship are connected. If we cooperate with God in the process of suffering, and depend on his grace and comfort, suffering will enable us to become purer and humbler people. It is the pure and humble who have truly learned to love God for who he is and to worship him most deeply.[34]

8

SERVANTHOOD AND HUMILITY

Suffering, as we have seen in the previous chapter, is a crucial part of servanthood. J. I. Packer has succinctly stated, "Suffering as defined (getting what one does not want while wanting what one does not get) is specified in Scripture as part of every Christian's calling. . . . Suffering must be expected and even valued by all believers without exception."[1] He goes on to say that we value suffering because our suffering produces character, glorifies God, and fulfills the law of harvest (i.e., before there is blessing there will first be suffering).[2] More specifically, suffering in servanthood also helps to produce humility in our lives as servants of Jesus.

Humility is an essential part of true Christian spirituality or maturity in Christ, as well as of servanthood. Servanthood and humility are inseparable. We cannot be servants or bondslaves of Jesus if we are not humble people! We read in Philippians 2:3–5: "Do nothing out of selfish ambition or vain conceit, but in humility consider others better than yourselves. Each of you should look not only to your own interests, but also to the interests of others. Your attitude should be the same as that of Christ Jesus."

Colossians 3:12 states, "Therefore, as God's chosen people, holy and dearly loved, clothe yourselves with compassion, kindness, humility, gentleness and patience." In 1 Peter 5:5–6 we read: "All of you, clothe yourselves with humility toward one another, because 'God opposes the proud but gives grace to the humble.' Humble yourselves, therefore, under God's mighty hand, that he may lift you up in due time." And Ephesians 4:2 says, "Be completely humble and gentle; be patient, bearing with one another in love."

There are many other Bible texts on humility. For example, Matthew 23:12 is seen by Peter Wagner as the foundational text for understanding humility: "Whoever exalts himself *will be humbled*, and whoever humbles himself *will be exalted* (emphasis added)."[3] Based on this text, and others such as Colossians 3:12 and 1 Peter 5:5–6, Wagner emphasizes that humility involves choosing to be humble: Being a humble person begins with a personal choice to humble ourselves.[4] He notes that the dictionary defines humble as "not proud or arrogant; modest; *to be humble although successful*."[5]

It is important to realize that while we can choose to walk humbly or to humble ourselves, we cannot directly manufacture or produce humility by our own self-efforts. We can choose the way of humility, the way of the cross—and so we should as servants of Jesus Christ. But ultimately, humility—or gentleness or meekness—is part of the fruit of the Holy Spirit (Gal. 5:22–23). We will grow in humility as we yield daily to the Spirit's control and are continually filled with the Spirit (Eph. 5:18).[6] Humility and true holiness in the Spirit are therefore intimately related. Andrew Murray, in his classic book *Humility*, written over a hundred years ago, noted: "The great test of whether the holiness we profess to seek or to attain is truth and life will be *whether it produces an increasing humility in us*."[7] Before I go further into humility and how it is formed or produced in our lives, we need to first consider the opposite of humility: pride. There are many biblical texts that speak against pride (e.g., Ps. 138:6; Prov. 6:16–17; 8:13; 16:5), which is sin (Prov. 21:4). Hence God hates pride and opposes the proud (Prov. 3:34; James 4:6; 1 Peter 5:5). There are also serious warnings about how pride precedes destruction or downfall (Prov. 16:18; 18:12).

Pride—Deadliest of the Seven Deadly Sins

The seven deadly sins—pride, envy, anger, sloth, greed, gluttony, and lust—were first assembled in this fashion as a list of attitudes and behaviors, all of which destroy and hence are "deadly," by Gregory the Great in the 6th century AD. He was bishop of Rome before he became pope in the year 590. Randy Rowland noted: "Gregory and others like him saw sin *as a distortion of love*. Perverted love results in pride, envy, rage (anger). Insufficient love results in sloth. Excessive love of things in this world leads to greed, gluttony, and lust."[8] Mark McMinn, in *Why Sin Matters*, pointed out that for centuries pride has been considered chief among the seven deadly sins.[9] Similarly, David Powlison has commented that pride has often been seen as the master sin or the deadliest of the seven deadly sins, and hence humility, or pride's opposite, is then the most foundational of the virtues.[10]

One of the best-known quotes about pride comes from C. S. Lewis in *Mere Christianity*: "Well, now, we have come to the center. According to Christian teachers, the essential vice, the utmost evil, is Pride. Unchastity, anger, grief, drunkenness, and all that, are mere fleabites in comparison: it was through Pride that the devil became the devil; Pride leads to every other vice; it is the complete anti-God state of mind."[11] Stuart Scott has defined pride as "the mindset of self, the pursuit of self-exaltation, a focus on the desire to control all things for self." [12]

Wagner notes that the dictionary defines pride as "a high or inordinate opinion of one's own dignity, importance, merit, or superiority, whether as cherished in the mind or as displayed in bearing, conduct, etc." Other words that describe aspects of pride include: arrogance, haughtiness, vainglory, conceit, egotism, stuck-up, vanity, and self-admiration.[13]

Servants of Jesus Christ will therefore be very careful about guarding against pride by yielding to the Holy Spirit's control and choosing daily to walk the way of humility with Jesus. Servanthood in humility will lead to true service. False servanthood in pride will lead to self-righteous service that is ultimately destructive to everyone and the community as well.

Characteristics of Pride

Scott has listed fifteen characteristics that can help us identify pride when it rears its ugly head in our hearts and lives: "(1) Being blind, unable to see pride; (2) Being unthankful; (3) Outbursts of anger, withdrawing, pouting, being moody or impatient; (4) Perfectionistic-type persons who want to be the best at everything. . . . They brag and talk about themselves all the time; (5) Seeking independence . . . They have to be their own boss; (6) Monopolizing conversations, being rigid, stubborn, headstrong, and intimidating; (7) Being consumed with what others might think of them, being [people] pleasers or [people] fearers; (8) Being devastated by criticism; (9) Not listening very well; (10) Being unteachable; (11) Being sarcastic, hurtful, jesting; (12) Wanting to be praised or to be coaxed to serve; (13) Being defensive; (14) Lacking in biblical prayer, in service to other people, and in sacrificial deeds of love; (15) Resisting authority, being disrespectful."[14]

Wagner provides a simpler and shorter description of what he calls "five signposts along the road to pride": (1) Yearning for praise and human accolades; (2) Keeping score (i.e., having a system for calculating how many self-defined, prestige-loaded "points" we have achieved); (3) Cultivating a creator complex (i.e., trying to change others and make them over in our own image);

(4) Rejoicing in others' failures and resenting others' successes; (5) Compulsively defending yourself against criticism.[15] He emphasizes the need to be filled constantly with the Holy Spirit and be sensitive to his convicting us of sin, righteousness, and judgment (John 16:8) so that we can recognize these signposts along the road to pride and turn away from them.[16]

Ken Blanchard and Phil Hodges have written about heart issues and the ego. At their Center for FaithWalk Leadership, they have come up with two simple definitions for the word EGO: It is either **E**dging **G**od **O**ut (referring to pride and being ego-centered or self-centered), or **E**xalting **G**od **O**nly (referring to humility and servanthood in leadership that glorifies God).[17]

Obsession with Self

There is a growing obsession with self and so-called self-help in our world today. This reflects how pride continues to work its evil effects on human beings, manifesting itself in the ever-increasing preoccupation and obsession with self. In an incisive and biblically-based critique of the self-help movement, Stephanie Forbes exposes today's obsession with Satan's oldest lie: *Help Your Self*, which is also the title of her book. She wrote: "Embedded in all the self-help messages I saw around me was the tacit assumption that human beings can and should seek their own fulfillment on their own terms. . . . Worst of all, this anti-Christian assumption has been making serious inroads into American Christianity. And very few people . . . appeared to notice."[18] She goes on to describe six major lies of the self-help movement today: "(1) I belong to myself; (2) I am entitled to a life of happiness and fulfillment; (3) I was born to greatness; (4) I can be as successful as I want if only . . . ; (5) I need to build my self-esteem; and (6) I need to learn positive self-talk."[19] Forbes suggests the following ways of resisting or withstanding such lies or half-truths of the enemy, Satan: Study the Bible, study church history, study church creeds, study apologetics, learn to accept paradox, evaluate Christian living books carefully and biblically, and always remember who our enemy is.[20] Carolyn Custis James has similarly emphasized that everyone needs solid, sound, biblically-based theology, because knowing God deeply or thinking seriously about what we believe about God makes a crucial difference when life and beliefs collide in the struggles and crucibles of our daily living.[21]

In reviewing the relevant contemporary social science research, psychologist McMinn noted that one of the clearest findings is that we are proud. He concluded: "The 'big' sins . . . are all derived from that abhorrent condition that reflects the disordered passions of our hearts: pride. We compare ourselves in an unrealistically favorable light with others. We attribute good outcomes to ourselves and bad outcomes to others. When others have misfortune, we blame them. And we justify our behavior by changing our opinions after we act. We love ourselves more than we love others. The damage report looks serious."[22] Similarly, Leslie Vernick, a licensed social worker, after examining secular research concluded that our difficulties in life are often due to thinking too highly and too much of ourselves: "Our problems in life usually don't stem from loving *ourselves* too little, but of *loving others and God* too little and ourselves too much."[23]

Part of choosing the way of humility, the way of the cross, is therefore to avoid the pathway of pride and the obsession with self. Let us now look more closely at what humility is all about. Let us then learn how to grow in humility as servants of Jesus Christ who live in and follow him all the way.

Humility—the Most Foundational Virtue

As Powlison has pointed out, if pride is the deadliest of the seven deadly sins and the master sin, then humility, the opposite of pride, is the most foundational of the virtues. Humility is essential in true Christian spirituality that is God-centered (not human-centered), based on objective truth (not subjective experience), and others-focused, as Gary Thomas has noted.[24] He wrote: "There is no truly Christian spirituality without humility. . . . Humility contains two truths—the lowliness of men and women and the greatness of God. . . . John the Baptist was the quintessential example of a humble servant of God. He was willing to serve humbly and obscurely in the desert while God readied him for his ministry. He spoke forcefully when God exalted him to become a famous and powerful prophet, but then he willingly handed his ministry over to Christ when the time was right. May God raise up many more such servants."[25] Humility is based on acknowledging our lowliness and the greatness of God. May we as servants of Jesus learn to be *humble* servants like John the Baptist!

Scott has provided a more detailed definition and explanation of what humility is all about: "The terms used in Hebrew and Greek for this character of humility all refer to bowing low, crouching—it's an attitude of heart, the real you. It means to bring low, to yield, to give way to God's way. Humility is the pursuit to magnify Christ by bowing low in complete adoration and obedience. It's the pursuit of magnifying Christ, not self, realizing that all goodness, honor, and glory comes from God, and needs to go to God."[26]

Characteristics of Humility

Scott has listed ten ways to display humility, or ten characteristics of humility: "(1) Focus on our Lord and Savior Jesus Christ as the author and perfecter of our faith; (2) Be overwhelmed by God's goodness; (3) Commune with God. Be extremely dependent upon God in prayer; (4) Serve others; (5) Obey God's revealed will in all things; (6) Learn from others; (7) Encourage others; (8) Pursue integrity in private as well as public life; (9) Deny self by assuming no rights, living unto Christ; (10) Think rightly or soberly about yourself while bowing low before God and others."[27] He mentions several biblical examples of humility such as Abraham (Gen. 13), Moses (Num. 12:3), John the Baptist (Luke 3:16), Mary, the mother of Jesus (Luke 1:46–48), the tax collector (Luke 18:13), and the apostle Paul who said to the Ephesian elders: "I served the Lord with great humility and with tears" (Acts 20:19).[28] He concludes: "Without humility there can be no true repentance, no true faith, no true love and obedience."[29] Without humility then, there can be no true servanthood in Christ!

Wagner similarly describes ten signposts along the road to humility: "(1) Carefully adhering to the biblical rules of submission; (2) Understanding the role of the Holy Spirit in your daily life (this is absolutely essential for achieving the true humility that God desires for us); (3) Discovering your spiritual gifts; (4) Knowing your place in the body of Christ; (5) Knowing the difference between your strengths and weaknesses; (6) Daring to be realistic about your successes and failures; (7) Taking risks; (8) Accepting praise but rejecting flattery; (9) Avoiding living in the achievements of the past; (10) Having the ability to pass on your glory (or credit) to others."[30]

Practicing and Growing in Humility

Now that we have covered much of the terrain of humility versus pride, we will examine how to practice and grow in humility. We begin by choosing to humble ourselves before God and others, and to depend on the Holy Spirit's help and power to transform us into humble servants. His deep work of grace *in* us is more foundational and important than what he will eventually do *through* us. Character always comes before competence: Who we *are* as servants of Jesus, our *being*, is more crucial than what we do in our service for him and others, our *doing*. The key issue, then, is *becoming* and *being* a truly *humble* person, practicing and growing in humility deep in our hearts. In the previously cited descriptions of the characteristics of humility, Scott and Wagner both included suggestions on how to practice humility.

Richard Foster also has much wisdom to offer us in this area of the practice and development of humility in our lives and ministries. He emphasizes the importance of having a more proper relationship with God by contemplating his greatness and goodness, and a more proper relationship with others by serving them. In so doing, we will end up with a more proper relationship with ourselves.[31]

Foster also puts in a strong word for the value of anonymity in the midst of our celebrity culture in which we try so hard to get noticed.[32] He points out the need to practice the spiritual discipline of "*secrecy*," as Dallas Willard calls it, or *anonymity* or *hiddeness,* which at its best will develop love and humility before God and others. Humility is an eventual result of such secrecy in our lives.

Foster suggests four practical ways to enter into secrecy that will help us grow in humility: "1. Look for one substantive act of service you can render this month. Then, do it without letting anyone know what you have done, or why. . . . 2. Become aware of the frantic efforts of people to advertise and certify themselves. . . . Be sure that you are observing simply as a way of learning and not with a condemning or judging spirit. . . . 3. As a . . . discipline intentionally look upon your work associates in the best possible light, even to the point of hoping they will do better and appear better than you. Whenever you are in a competitive situation, pray that they will be more outstanding, more praised, and more used of God than yourself. 4. In order to keep from turning this work of hiddenness into an absurdity or, worse yet, into a soul-killing legalism, learn to receive praise and recognition well. . . . When you are complimented, learn to say, 'Thank you.'"[33]

In the previous chapter, I noted other examples of spiritual disciplines besides secrecy that Nelson has described as voluntary behaviors of brokenness that can help us grow in humility: solitude, silence, fasting, simplicity, chastity, sacrifice, study, prolonged prayer, celebration, service, fellowship, confession, and submission. However, the Lord often uses involuntary brokenness, and especially experiences of suffering, to help us grow in humility and deeper Christlike love. Although humility and humiliation are not synonymous, growing in humility will sooner or later include some experiences of humiliation or humbling! As we learn to value suffering and embrace brokenness, including even humiliating or humbling experiences, we will grow in humility and true servanthood.

Rory Noland, music director for many years at Willow Creek Community Church, has emphasized the need for Christians with artistic temperaments to learn to be servants or humble artists: to choose servanthood versus stardom. He suggests the following ways to embrace humility as an artist who is a true servant of Jesus: "Humble yourself before God, humble yourself before others, die to your desire to be the greatest, focus on people, remember that the message is more important, examine your motivation, die to selfishness, and remember that ministry is a privilege."[34]

Philip Kenneson described three ways of cultivating gentleness or humility in the midst of a society marked by aggression and self-promotion: *altering our posture through prayer* as we bow humbly before God and pray for others including our enemies; *learning to yield* to others and admit our mistakes or wrongs; and *hanging out with those of "no account,"* with genuine acts of hospitality (because hospitality is intimately connected to humility), including being with, and really listening to, children.[35]

Humility: Faith to Face Failure

One particularly crucial aspect of humility and growing in humility is having the faith to face failure. Failure is a bad word in an achievement-oriented and success-obsessed society like America. Yet failure experiences that can be humiliating but also humbling, and learning from that failure, are crucial ways of growing in humility. Vernon Grounds wrote some powerful words years ago on this very topic:

> Most of us will work without ever becoming well-known. Do we have faith to face failure? Do we really believe that worldly success is wood, hay, and stubble? We need to remember how often the Church will judge us the way the world does. Before anyone decides on a full-time ministry for example, they must realize that God may be calling him or her to a ministry of tedious mediocrity. Regardless, God's approval is the most important. It is far more important to follow God's blueprint for your life than to be another Billy Graham . . . or Robert Schuller, or Bill Bright. Each of us needs the faith to cling to biblical principles of success despite possible worldly failure. And each of us must have the faith to keep serving even if unappreciated, unsung, and unapplauded—in short, we need the faith to face failure.[36]

Before I share a few examples of humble servanthood, let me reiterate how central humility is in the Christian life. Simon Chan put it this way: "If pride is the cardinal sin, humility is the only way forward. Scripture counsels humility (James 4:6; 1 Peter 5:5–6) and warns against having too high an estimate of oneself (Rom. 12:3). Calvin underscores the importance of humility: 'if you ask me concerning the precepts of the Christian religion, first, second, third, and always I would answer, "Humility".'"[37]

Examples of Humble Servanthood

As we saw in the previous chapter, there are countless examples of humble servants of Jesus Christ who also end up as suffering servants. However, let me share a few examples that will encourage us as servants of Christ to continue to grow in humility.

I would like to begin by briefly sharing about my own mother, partly because I know she would be the last person to share about herself. She is almost eighty and still living in Singapore, my country of origin. She has never been to school, and is therefore uneducated and illiterate. She cannot read or write in any language. Yet, she lovingly and sacrificially raised seven children. In 1976, my father passed away after his second stroke in a year, so my mother has been a widow for three decades. She has also had much suffering in her life, including a number of health problems as she has grown older. After about twenty-eight years of sharing Christ and his love with her, on one of my trips back to Singapore my mother finally prayed with me to accept Jesus into her heart. I was overjoyed. Although she is struggling with her growth in faith, my mother is a good example of a humble person. Previously, whenever I told her about the latest book I had written, her usual reply was "Don't write any more. Don't overstrain yourself. Make sure you take good care of your health and your family!" Her loving concern for me and my well-being, as well as for my family, is obvious. Her complete lack of concern for greatness or success or publications is even more obvious. Her humility continues to be used by the Lord to help me walk the way of the cross, the way of humility and true servanthood. When I am tempted with pride because of my accomplishments or achievements, the Lord often reminds me of my mom—and her humility. And I often end up in tears and in prayer, confessing my pride to the Lord, choosing to humble myself before him and yield to the Holy Spirit afresh, to walk the way of humility and servanthood again.

In a recent telephone conversation with my mother in which I told her about my writing of this book on servanthood, she for the first time got excited and was glad I was writing such a book! I was deeply touched and blessed by her response. I thanked her again for her example of humility and loving servanthood, and we rejoiced that it is Jesus who calls us to such a life and empowers us, by the Holy Spirit, to live such a lifestyle.

There are also examples of humble servants of the Lord who have had much so-called success in their ministries but who never forget that it is the Lord who is great, not themselves. They have learned to simply do things for a great God, and not so much to do great things for God! One such example is Rick Warren, well-known author and senior pastor of Saddleback Church in Lake Forest, California, with 15,000 members plus about 5,000 visitors who attend weekend services. He was featured in an article in a recent issue of *Time* (March 29, 2004). Sonja Steptoe, author of the article, wrote:

> Warren might just be, as *Christianity Today* has declared, America's most influential pastor . . . Remarkably, Warren has managed to spread his approach to the gospel without extensive national media coverage or a TV ministry. . . . "Too many ministers start out as servants and end up as celebrities," he says. "I want to use my influence to do some good, and I can get more done out of the limelight." . . . In person, Warren, an affable, bespectacled bear of a man, is as unadorned and low-key as the plainspoken prose of his books. . . . "From the beginning, I was impressed by his humility," says Patricia Miller, who has attended Saddleback since 1998. . . . In 2003, with royalties from the Purpose-Driven product line pouring in, Warren stopped taking his $110,000 salary from Saddleback and refunded all the money the church had paid him over the years . . . he keeps only 10% of the book royalties and gives the rest away to Saddleback and the charitable foundation he and Kay established to supplement the church's mission projects, which include fighting poverty, illiteracy and disease—especially AIDS—here and abroad.[38]

Another example of humble servanthood can be found in songwriter Darlene Zschech (pronounced "check"), who leads worship every week at Hillsong Church in Sydney, Australia, with 15,000 members. In a recent interview with her, Leigh DeVore wrote: "She believes the primary pitfall of a Christian leader is self-admiration. That's why she stresses the need to always maintain the heart of a servant. 'I think for every Christian leader your admiration is your worst enemy,' she says. 'I think you need to be always getting your hands dirty, serving. You don't graduate from a life of service. The price for us is higher.'"[39]

Peter Wagner chose John Stott of England as another current-day example of humility. Wagner wrote: "I am choosing Stott because he and I have known each other for 30 years. . . . Few Christian leaders have gained as much admiration and respect from such a broad spectrum in the evangelical community as has John Stott. How did Stott arrive at such an enviable position? John Yates, who served for several years as Stott's study assistant, can answer this question better than most. In a recent article, Yates asserts that 'a key characteristic of John Stott [is] his disarming humility.'"[40]

There are other examples of famous yet humble servants of the Lord such as Mother Teresa, who was bestowed the Nobel Peace Prize in 1979, and Bill Bright, who was awarded the Templeton Prize for Progress in Religion in 1996. Then there is Billy Graham. I have been deeply blessed by the example of his life and ministry as the most influential and well-known evangelist of the twentieth century and even up till today. Shortly after August 1968, when I became a Christian as a young teenager in Singapore, I read John Pollock's biography of Billy Graham. Even then, over three and a half decades ago, his world-wide evangelistic ministry had already impacted many people. God stirred up the gift of evangelism in my young heart and gave me the compassionate heart of Jesus for the lost, by inspiring me and anointing me through Billy Graham's example.

While writing this book, I attended the last day of the Greater Los Angeles Billy Graham Crusade, held November 18–21, 2004, at the Rose Bowl. More than 80,000 people were present that day. I wept several times as I listened to the frail 86-year-old Graham preach again the old, old story, but always so ever new and powerful, of Jesus and his love for lost sinners. During the altar call, 3,400 came forward to commit their lives to Christ. The *Pasadena Star-News* reported on Monday, November, 22, 2004 (p. A4), that about 312,500 people attended the four-day crusade which marked the 55th anniversary of Graham's initial Los Angeles campaign in 1949. The latest statistics from the Greater Los Angeles Billy Graham Crusade office (December 17, 2004) stated that 14,160 people came forward, with 1,621 of them from language groups other than English.

The following quotes, from an excellent pictorial book on Billy Graham by Russ Busby,[41] reflect the deep faith, integrity, and humility of this loving servant of Jesus Christ, who has preached in person to over 100 million people, and reached more than two billion people through radio, television, and satellite broadcasts:

> I would put Billy in line with the Wesleys and Saint Augustine and Francis of Assisi. He's in that league. And what's extraordinary is that he doesn't seem to know it. He doesn't want a Graham church. He is more interested in sharing the Lord than in grabbing the limelight. He wants to be a servant of the church, to challenge and spark the churches to be what they must become: the evangelizing agents of God and His Word. But there's no doubt about it: he is the most spiritually productive servant of God in our time.
>
> —Reverend Maurice Wood, bishop of Norwich and member of Britain's House of Lords[42]

> He has walked with royalty and received unprecedented media attention for over four decades but is still something of a small-town boy, astonished that anyone would think of him as special. In a profession tainted by scandal, he stands out as the clearly identified exemplar of clean-living integrity.
>
> —Bill Martin, author of *A Prophet with Honor: The Billy Graham Story*[43]

> All that I have been able to do I owe to Jesus Christ. When you honor me you are really honoring Him. Any honors I have received I accept with a sense of inadequacy and humility and I will reserve the right to hand all of these someday to Christ when I see him face-to-face.
>
> —Billy Graham[44]

Finally, there are many examples of humble servants of Christ who serve others quietly and oftentimes in hidden ways. Rory Noland told the story of one such person, John Allen, who discipled him in the early days of his ministry. Noland learned about true servanthood from Allen, who had a servant's heart as he helped people as a handyman. He fixed broken water heaters, leaky pipes, and worn-down drywall and did yard work for Noland, and he fasted and prayed with him when major decisions had to be made in his life. Allen was a real servant who experienced deep joy in serving an audience of One.[45] I too know of a gifted handyman who goes about quietly serving others in the church and in many homes, fixing things without charge. I am a terrible handyman, and I have been deeply blessed and helped by this humble servant of Christ who has fixed things in our home, as he has done for so many others and for our church. Noland is therefore right on when he asserts: "The ultimate test of servanthood is whether you can be content to serve an audience of One, when it's OK to serve in anonymity, when you can throw yourself into a bit part, when you no longer live for the approval of others, when the size of your audience doesn't matter anymore, and when the size of the role you play is less important than being faithful and obedient."[46]

Brennan Manning reminds us, however, that there is one more crucial step that is essential in the development of true humility: forgiveness and the acceptance of others, letting go of our resentments and grudges against others who may have offended or hurt us. He writes: "Suffering alone does not produce a prayerful spirit.

Humiliation alone does not foster humility. Desolation alone does not guarantee the increase of faith. . . . We can still be wallowing in self-pity and rebellion, pride or apathy, and the last state will be worse than the first. . . . One further crucial step in the process of ego-slaying remains. The most characteristic feature of the humility of Jesus is his forgiveness and acceptance of others. . . . The surest sign of union with the crucified Christ is our forgiveness of those who have perpetuated injustices against us."[47]

Let me end this chapter by sharing with you the benediction that Brennan Manning gave after his general session address at the National Pastors Convention held in San Diego in March 2004, based on the benediction he received from his spiritual director. It went something like this: "May all your expectations be frustrated, all your plans be thwarted, all your dreams be shattered, all your desires be withered into nothingness, so that you may know the powerlessness and poverty of a child, and experience and rest in the love of God the Father, Son, and Holy Spirit, for you!" Amen.

9

Servanthood and Rest

Servanthood and suffering. Servanthood and humility. It doesn't sound like servanthood is connected at all to rest, does it? Yet, the truth is that servanthood is foundational to experiencing the rest Jesus promised us in him (Matt. 11:28–30): the rest of his grace, and the grace of his rest. Remember Brennan Manning's benediction? It is only when our expectations are frustrated, our plans thwarted, our dreams shattered, and our desires withered into nothingness that we know firsthand the powerlessness and poverty of a child, and hence experience and *rest* in the love of God for us! In the brokenness of true servanthood, deep rest in the Lord can be experienced. There is servanthood and rest.

Our attitudes affect our feelings and behavior. Attitudes of pride, arrogance, and entitlement can rob us of God's rest and peace. An attitude of servanthood, on the other hand, enables us, by the power of the Holy Spirit, to serve the Lord with humility and hiddenness and with much rest and rejoicing in him.[1] Servanthood is therefore a crucial means of grace to enter more deeply into God's rest for us in Christ.

Defining Rest

Rest can be defined as "a state of peace, contentment, serenity, refreshment, stillness, tranquility, or calm."[2] It is usually described as having four dimensions or aspects: physical rest, emotional rest, relational rest, and spiritual rest. These four types of rest are actually interrelated. Our eventual experience of rest is a holistic one, integrating all these dimensions of rest as the *shalom* or peace of God that transcends all understanding (Phil. 4:7).[3]

In the *physical* area, there are many people today who suffer from heart disease and other stress-related conditions such as addictions, panic attacks, exhaustion, insomnia, high blood pressure, muscle tension, and headaches. Our tired and worn-out bodies, that result from the constant overload and hectic schedules of hurried and harried lifestyles, yearn for physical rest. While physical rest may not be the most important aspect of the rest we need, it is nonetheless an essential type of rest for us. Physical rest requires time for leisure and sleep (at least 7 to 8 hours a night!), including taking a Sabbath day off every week. It also involves regular exercise, good nutrition, and learning at least one good relaxation technique as part of effective stress management.

In the *emotional* area, many of us have a hard time coping with the demands and stresses of our over-busy lives in today's high-speed technological world. We may experience emotional struggles such as anxiety, panic, fear, depression, confusion, and feeling overwhelmed or trapped. We long for emotional rest from our overstimulated and drained emotions; we yearn for peace, quiet, contentment, and serenity. Mental or intellectual rest is part of emotional rest. Our emotions can relax when our minds are tranquil and at rest. Emotional rest is also deepened by spiritual rest.

In the *relational* or interpersonal area, we often experience stress and turmoil that come from difficult or broken relationships, unresolved conflicts, bitterness, misunderstandings, gossip, and even betrayal and breach of trust. We long therefore for relational rest: for peace and harmony in our relationships with one another, whether in our homes, churches, schools, workplaces, or the larger community and society in which we live. Such relational rest is often found in caring and loving relationships with others. Deep friendships and fellowship with each other, founded on prayer, open sharing, forgiveness, support, and accountability—spiritual community—will help us experience more relational rest and wholeness.

In the *spiritual* area, we may struggle with doubt, confusion, disappointment with God and co-workers in the ministry, guilt, emptiness, dryness, and despair. We all long for spiritual rest deep within our souls. We want to experience the peace of God that transcends all understanding (Phil. 4:7), that comes from praying with thanksgiving (Phil. 4:6) and casting all our anxiety on him (1 Peter 5:7). True spiritual rest, or supernatural peace, comes ultimately from growing in our intimate relationship of love with Jesus Christ, our best friend (see Matt. 11:28–30).

Ways of Experiencing Rest

I have already mentioned servanthood as one crucial means of experiencing more deeply God's rest that is first spiritual rest but also includes physical rest, emotional rest, and relational rest. In a previous book, *Rest*, I have described nine major ways (including servanthood) of experiencing rest. I will briefly review and summarize them here. They are Shepherd-centeredness, Spirit-filled surrender, solitude and silence, simplicity, Sabbath, sleep, spiritual community, servanthood, and stress management from a biblical perspective.[4]

Shepherd-centeredness is foundational to experiencing rest. It refers to first making the Lord Jesus our own Shepherd (Psalm 23), our personal Lord and Savior, by praying to receive him into our hearts by simple faith in him who loves us and gave himself for us (Gal. 2:20). Jesus is the "good shepherd" (John 10:11, 14) who gave his life for his sheep by dying on the cross for our sins, the "great Shepherd" of the sheep (Heb. 13:20) who keeps caring for us, and the "Chief Shepherd" (1 Peter 5:4) who will return soon from heaven with eternal rewards for his faithful servants. Shepherd-centeredness also means abiding, remaining, or dwelling in Christ (John 15:5), our best friend in an intimate, deep, loving relationship. It involves Walking with Jesus Daily! Finally, Shepherd-centeredness involves resting in Jesus through surrender to him in meekness and humility.

Spirit-filled surrender emphasizes the need to yield, submit, or surrender our lives fully to God, to the Lordship of Christ (Col. 2:6), and to the control and filling of the Holy Spirit (1 Cor. 6:19–20; Eph. 5:18). It includes surrendering our sin (confessing our sins and pursuing holiness and hatred of sin by the Spirit's power); yielding every area of our lives whether our time, talents (gifts or skills), treasure (money and possessions), or relationships; and giving ourselves fully to the Lord, in love, obedience, gratitude, and worship of him alone. Rest comes to the servant who is fully surrendered to the Lord and filled with the Holy Spirit whose fruit includes peace.

Solitude and silence are crucial spiritual disciplines already mentioned earlier in this book. They are essential behaviors of brokenness that enable us, by the power of the Holy Spirit, to rest more deeply and fully in the Lord. Solitude refers to time spent alone with God, intentionally withdrawing from all human interaction or contact. Silence in solitude refers to the absence of noise, words, speech, or other sounds including music. Silence is especially important for us to practice as a key aspect of solitude. We live in a noisy and over-stimulated world. Even our times of worship, whether individually or corporately, privately or publicly, are filled with music or other less-pleasant sounds. The still small voice of God, or his gentle whispers of love (cf. 1 Kings 19:11–13), cannot be discerned and heard in the midst of such noise. Silence is definitely needed, in our solitude, to hear God more clearly and rest in him more deeply. True servants of Jesus have learned to make solitude, and especially silence, a regular part of their daily lives as they rest in him.

Simplicity is another way of experiencing rest. It is a spiritual discipline that can be described as "practicing a lifestyle free of excess, greed, and covetousness so that we can draw closer to God and reach out to others in compassionate service. As we enter into simplicity, the Holy Spirit empowers us to seek first the Kingdom of God, to keep our eyes on Jesus, and to live free of crippling anxiety and lust for money."[5] Recently, the number of both Christian and secular books on simplicity has increased dramatically, reflecting people's yearning for a simpler lifestyle, for rest and a more contented life. Richard Foster has written an excellent book on simplicity entitled *Freedom of Simplicity*, emphasizing that simplicity leads to freedom to live the abundant life that Christ has given us his servants and disciples, including knowing his peace and rest. He describes three major types of simplicity: *Inward simplicity* focuses on the divine center within our hearts and on holy obedience. *Outward simplicity* involves taking gradual steps toward living a simpler lifestyle of giving, service, and sacrifice, and uncluttering our lives of unnecessary possessions, identifying with the poor. Finally, *corporate simplicity*, in both the church and in the world, deals with tough issues of economics, world hunger, and international trade.[6]

Sabbath, or keeping the Sabbath, is another means of entering more deeply into God's rest. Many Christians today ignore God's command to keep the Sabbath holy (Exod. 20:8–11, Deut. 5:15): one day a week to cease from work, to rest, and to worship God. In trying not to be legalistic (Mark 2:27–28), we end up disobeying God's commandment, thinking that it is only a good idea or suggestion! As true servants of Jesus, we learn to keep the Sabbath each week, because we want to be obedient to God's will and commands. We experience God's rest and peace more fully as we willingly cease from work, worship God, and rest once a week on our Sabbath day (which does not have to be on a Sunday or Saturday). Marva Dawn has written an excellent book on keeping the Sabbath wholly, by ceasing, resting, embracing, and feasting in various ways once a week.[7]

Sleep is a way of experiencing rest. Not just physical rest, but also emotional, relational, and spiritual rest! It is God's way of restoring us as whole persons. Deep and sound sleep is a blessing from the Lord, as he grants sleep to those he loves (Ps. 127:2). Arch Hart, former dean of the Graduate School of Psychology at Fuller Theological Seminary, has emphasized the need to have adequate sleep. He is convinced that most of us need one or two more hours of sleep each night than what we are currently getting.[8] More recent research suggests that there are individual differences in how much sleep each of us needs, but most of us need seven to eight hours of sleep each night. It is interesting to note that three recent studies, including one published in the February 2004 issue of the journal *Sleep*, have reported similar results showing that people who sleep about seven hours a night live the longest (*USA Today*, Feb. 9, 2004, 4D).[9] Too much or too little sleep is therefore not good for us! It is important for us, as servants of Jesus who tend to be sacrificial in our service of others for his sake, to have enough sleep. Many pastors and other servants of the Lord are sleep-deprived, often having only four or five hours of sleep each night because of the demands of ministry and the needs of the people being served. We need to have sufficient sleep to experience adequate rest. Taking naps can also be helpful and restful, as long as we do not suffer from insomnia or have difficulty sleeping at night. Hart therefore asserts: "There is no greater God-given gift that can help us maintain a tranquil, non-anxious existence than sleep. Sleep is one of the most powerful healing mechanisms given to us. . . . Sleep simply is the best antidote for stress, and therefore, for anxiety as well. Sleep enhances our natural tranquilizers and reverses the effects of the damage we do to ourselves through overstress."[10]

Spiritual community is another means of experiencing rest, especially relational rest. Since American Christianity, following American culture in general, tends to be highly individualistic and even self-obsessed, it is important for servants of Jesus to realize that the Christian faith is God-centered and others-oriented, not self-focused. Although we do end up finding our true self in Christ, Christian faith and spiritual growth are not self-obsessed. According to M. Robert Mulholland, Jr., spiritual formation is "*a process of being conformed to the image of Christ for the sake of others*."[11] Spiritual community then becomes crucial for our growing and maturing together in fellowship and friendship in Christ. Such spiritual community involves deep, connecting, loving spiritual friendships or relationships that enable us to experience God's rest and peace from others, as well as to be channels of his peace and rest to others. Spiritual community includes Christian fellowship in church or small groups;[12] family relationships;[13] spiritual friendships;[14] and spiritual direction or mentoring;[15] where we can engage in what Larry Crabb recently termed "soultalk."[16] Soultalk is deep, supernatural or spiritual conversation connecting people soul to soul, and connecting each other to God, by the presence and power of the Holy Spirit. Servants of Jesus will be deeply involved in spiritual community as they live and serve in God-centered and others-focused ways. Such spiritual community is a significant means of spiritual growth and experiencing God's peace and rest, for the sake of others.

Servanthood itself is a way or means of entering more deeply into God's rest. The very nature or essence of true servanthood in Christ is characterized by brokenness, humility, hiddenness, obedience, love, and God-centeredness, with a focus on ministering to others as the Lord leads. Such a servant heart or servant attitude will therefore be a strong antidote to pride and all of its ugly manifestations that take away rest and God's peace: competitiveness, arrogance, entitlement, self-absorption and self-obsession, envy or jealousy, manipulative control of others, resentment, and bitterness. Freedom from the need to have other people's approval and praise, and hence from the need to be the great hero or heroine (the "Messiah" complex), in true servanthood will produce much rest and peace in the Spirit. Servanthood that is founded on faithfulness rather than on worldly success, with the faith to face and even embrace failure, rejection, and persecution, will lead to deep rest and peace in the Lord, as well as deep joy!

Stress management from a biblical perspective will also help us to enter more fully into God's rest. Servants of Jesus are particularly in danger of overstress and burnout, since sacrificial service to others is often part and parcel of a servant's life. Ajith Fernando has pointed out that we are not only servants of God or of Christ (1 Cor. 4:1), but we are also servants of those to whom we are ministering (2 Cor. 4:5; cf. 1 Cor. 9:19). He therefore defines servanthood as "the commitment to do all we can for the welfare of the people whose servants we are."[17] Of course, our first commitment is to the Lord Jesus Christ who will lead us to minister appropriately in servanthood and not servitude. But even in servanthood, sacrifice is often involved. Servants of Jesus will manage stress better and prevent burnout if they focus on true success from God's viewpoint: Christlike agape love (John 13:34–35; 1 Cor. 13:1–8), servanthood and humility (Matt. 20:25–27), faithfulness (Matt. 25:21), obedience to God and his Word (Josh. 1:7–9; 1 Sam. 15:22; Matt. 7:24–29), vulnerability and strength in weakness (2 Cor. 12:9–10), doing our best for the Lord (Col. 3:23), and becoming more like Jesus (Rom. 8:29). There are also several good books on stress management written from a Christian, biblical perspective.[18] They include many helpful and practical, biblically based suggestions for effectively managing stress and preventing burnout. For example, Arch Hart has provided the following guidelines: (1) set boundaries or limits in your life; (2) resolve conflicts quickly; (3)

complete unpleasant tasks first; (4) "inoculate" yourself against stress by dealing with small amounts of stress in an effective way; (5) firmly set up "recovery times" after particular periods of stress; (6) minimize your level of adrenaline arousal; (7) have open and healthy relationships; (8) learn to say no and give yourself a break; (9) postpone making major decisions in times of stress; (10) use spiritual resources for stress-busting.[19]

In the recently revised and expanded edition of *Coping with Depression*, John Ortberg and I described several helpful ways of coping effectively with depression, the majority of which are also relevant for effectively managing stress and anxiety. They include: *inner healing prayer* for painful memories; *learning to be assertive* (for example, learning to say no to unreasonable demands from people without feeling guilty); *relaxation and coping skills* such as those used in stress-inoculation training, like *slow, deep breathing* (take in a slow deep breath, hold it for a few seconds, then breathe out slowly), *calming self-talk* (for example, saying to yourself, "Just relax, take it easy, allow the tension to unwind. With God's help, I can handle this."), and *pleasant imagery* (for example, imagining lying on the beach or visualizing a beautiful sunset or sunrise); *listening to music* that is uplifting or soothing; *taking care of the body* by practicing good nutrition, regular exercise, and getting sufficient sleep; *cognitive restructuring* of negative, unbiblical, extreme, irrational thinking into more biblical, realistic, reasonable thinking; *prayer with thanksgiving* (Phil. 4:6–7); *use of humor* (Prov. 15:15; 17:22); *self-help reading* of the right kind, written from a biblical perspective; and *contemplative prayer and meditation on Scripture* (Ps. 119:15, 97).[20]

Maintaining Healthy Boundaries

Rory Noland has emphasized the need for servants of Jesus, especially Christian artists, to have healthy boundaries. He wrote: "Now let me ask you: Is it possible to serve too much? Can one overdo this serving thing? The answer is yes. You can spend too much time at church and neglect your family, your health, and even your relationship with the Lord. That's a real shame because it does not glorify God to burn out on ministry. You have to set healthy boundaries. Maintaining healthy boundaries involves having your priorities in place, resulting in the freedom to say yes but not the fear to say no. If you expect to serve the Lord for any length of time, you've got to develop healthy boundaries. We all have to know how and when to say no, long before we reach personal crisis."[21]

Henry Cloud and John Townsend, both well-known Christian psychologists, have written several helpful books on boundaries (keeping healthy limits) that are relevant to servanthood and rest.[22]

Essentials of Highly Healthy People

Recently, Walt Larimore, a family physician and now vice president of medical outreach for Focus on the Family, wrote a book with Traci Mullins titled *10 Essentials of Highly Healthy People*. Learning to be highly healthy people as servants of Jesus will definitely help us to experience more holistic well-being and rest. Larimore provides guidance for doing a self-assessment of your health in four major areas—physical, emotional, relational, and spiritual—which are also the dimensions of rest that we have briefly covered in this chapter. He then explains and describes the following ten essentials of highly healthy people who have holistic well-being and vitality, based on reliable medical research and biblical principles: (1) *The essential of balance*—set a wise balance in your life; (2) *The essential of self-care*—be proactive in preventing disease; (3) *The essential of forgiveness*—practice acceptance and letting go; (4) *The essential of reducing SADness* (Stress, Anxiety, and Depression)—lighten your load; (5) *The essential of relationships*—avoiding loneliness; (6) *The essential of spiritual well-being*—cultivate a true spirituality; (7) *The essential of a positive self-image*—see yourself as your Creator sees you (but with humility and realistic self-acceptance, based on God's love and grace); (8) *The essential of discovering your destiny*—nurture your hopes and dreams (But first, the Lord may need to shatter our self-centered hopes and dreams in order to reveal hopes and dreams that are aligned to his will for us!); (9) *The essential of personal responsibility*—be your own health-care quarterback; and (10) *The essential of teamwork*—team up with winning health-care providers.[23]

In this chapter, we have seen how we can enter into God's rest by trust and faith in Christ. We have also learned of various ways of experiencing more of God's peace and rest in a restless and stressful world. However, as disciples and servants of Jesus, we realize that, ultimately, perfect peace and everlasting rest can only be ours in heaven (Rev. 21:4). We will have to wait till then. We wait, with deep hope and anticipatory joy, to see the Lord face to face. Meanwhile, we continue to serve our best friend and walk with Jesus daily in his rest and peace: a foretaste of heaven to come!

10

Servant Evangelism and Warfare

True servants of Jesus, filled with the Holy Spirit, will manifest the fruit of the Spirit: love, joy, peace, patience, kindness, goodness, faithfulness, gentleness (humility or meekness), and self-control (Gal. 5:22–23). Servants of Christ will therefore be filled with kindness. Part of true service involves doing acts of kindness to bless and benefit others, to help them in their need.

Kindness—Essential Fruit

Philip Kenneson wrote the following about cultivating the fruit of kindness in the midst of self-sufficiency in our society: "Kindness is a particular manifestation of love's other-directedness. Kindness seems to manifest itself as a certain way of being helpful to those who need help. Such a helpfulness stems first of all from God's helpfulness, of which the Christian is imminently mindful. . . . This fruit by its very character, therefore, is one of the most outwardly *visible* fruit of the Christian life . . . we regard people as kind because they go out of their way, often quietly and without fanfare, to engage in kind actions. Nitty-gritty, concrete, everyday kinds of actions."[1]

However, servanthood that is characterized by this spiritual fruit of kindness is not about doing or practicing "random acts of kindness" as car bumper stickers and other signs and billboards have been challenging us to do for some years now. Such random acts of kindness should really be called "random acts of niceness,"[2] not kindness, as Steve Sjogren has pointed out. There is nothing random or accidental about kindness as a fruit of the Holy Spirit (Gal. 5:22–23)! The Holy Spirit substantially and intentionally produces the fruit of kindness in us as we yield to him and nurture our spiritual lives by walking with God daily and practicing the spiritual disciplines as disciplines of the Holy Spirit. Kindness has been defined by Sjogren as "*practical acts of mercy done by followers of Jesus who are inspired by the Holy Spirit to see others through the eyes of God*. Paul writes that 'the kindness of God leads us to repentance' (Rom. 2:4). The Bible seems to distinguish between the divine quality of kindness and the human quality of niceness."[3]

In a similar vein, Kenneson also critiques the idea of simply doing random acts of "kindness" (or niceness). The main limitation of such acts, according to him, is that genuine other-directedness is lacking—we feel good about doing these random acts of "kindness," regardless of what the recipients may really need.[4]

Kenneson suggests three major ways in which true kindness can be cultivated in our lives in the Spirit as Christians.[5] The first is in *remembering our story*, especially as undeserved recipients of God's great kindness and matchless grace in Jesus Christ and his sacrificial love for us on the cross. We therefore gather regularly for worship of God, being constantly reminded, because we need to be, of our utter dependency on God and how he gloriously works through our human weakness. The second is in *nurturing connections*, especially as members of the body of Christ, who see one another as precious gifts of God to each other. We are therefore challenged to give up our self-sufficiency and autonomy. We are empowered by the Holy Spirit instead to become true servants to one another in mutual service for the building up of the body of Christ. The giving and receiving of acts of kindness (not random acts of niceness!) are crucial aspects of such servanthood. The third is in *listening to one another*.[6] In order to nurture deeper and more loving relationships with each other, to connect with one another in the Spirit in the depths of our soul, we need to listen to one another carefully and attentively. This kind of listening will help us to discern and know each other's deepest needs and to respond lovingly and appropriately to such needs with Spirit-filled acts of kindness that are truly other-directed. In fact, listening itself is a kindness we can give to others in a self-obsessed world where very few people are heard deeply enough to feel understood.

Servant Evangelism and Warfare

Sjogren wrote about "servant evangelism" over a decade ago. In describing this refreshing approach to sharing the love of Jesus with others, he gave concrete examples such as giving free car washes, cleaning toilets, and feeding parking meters before they expire (although more recently it may be illegal in some cities to do this!). Servant evangelism consists of deeds of love plus words of love plus adequate time.[7] It is kindness concretely manifested to meet specific needs of others because of Jesus Christ.

Sjogren has therefore concluded: "Small things done with great love can change the world."[8] Based on servant evangelism, he went on to define "servant warfare" as "*using the power of kindness to penetrate the spiritually darkened hearts of people with the love of God.*"[9] In the last few decades, much has been written, discussed, and debated on spiritual warfare,[10] as well as on the powerful ministry of the Holy Spirit.[11] We need to use the full armor of God in spiritual warfare, in the power and presence of the Holy Spirit, against the devil and the demonic powers of evil (Eph. 6:10–18; also see 1 Peter 5:8–9), especially the sword of the Spirit, which is the Word of God (Eph. 6:17), and prayer in the Spirit (Eph. 6:18). Most Christians know about spiritual warfare and the need to use the Word of God and prayer, as well as the other aspects of the full armor of God, to resist and overcome evil. We also know that he who is in us is greater than he who is in the world, the devil (1 John 4:4). However, many of us may not realize that *kindness* can be a powerful and effective weapon of spiritual warfare! When the fruit of kindness is expressed in doing small things with great love for the people around us, evil is broken and the powerful light of Jesus shines into the spiritually darkened hearts of those who do not yet know Jesus and his love. Such servant evangelism and servant warfare, as Sjogren has pointed out, will help people to come to know Jesus as their personal Lord and Savior, as their best friend.

As servants of Jesus, we will have his heart of love and compassion for the lost (Luke 19:10). By the power of the Holy Spirit (Acts 1:8), we will obey the Great Commandment to love God and to love our neighbor as ourselves (Mark 12:30–31) and the Great Commission to go and make disciples of all nations (Matt. 28:18–20), or to go into all the world and preach the good news to all creation (Mark 16:15). We will say, like the apostle Paul: "Though I am free and belong to no man, I make myself a slave to everyone, to win as many as possible. . . . To the weak I became weak, to win the weak. I have become all things to all men so that by all means I might save some" (1 Cor. 9:19, 22). We become servants to everyone, as servants of Jesus, in flexible, sensitive, loving outreach, to bring as many people to Christ as possible. True servanthood ultimately involves servant evangelism and servant warfare. It involves evangelism and world missions. As David Shibley put it: "What I am urging upon all of us is that we so freshly fall in love with Jesus Christ that what is precious to Him becomes precious to us and what is priority for Him becomes priority for us. Jesus is very clear about what that is. He said, 'The Son of man has come to seek and to save that which was lost' (Luke 19:10, NKJV)."[12]

Serving our best friend involves first knowing him and then falling in love with him over and over again! Knowing and loving the Lord come first before serving him. When we really know him and his love for us, our top priority is to love him and serve him in servant evangelism because his top priority is to seek and save the lost for whom he lovingly and sacrificially died and rose again. It is crucial to realize that it is the Holy Spirit who empowers and enables us to be witnesses of Jesus to the ends of the earth (Acts 1:8) with *kindness*, the hallmark of servant evangelism. The secret of effective witness is therefore to be filled with the Holy Spirit who leads us into divine appointments with people who need to personally know Jesus Christ.[13] Although some of us may be spiritually gifted as evangelists (Eph. 4:11), *all* of us as Christians and servants of Jesus have been called and empowered by the Spirit to be witnesses for Christ (Acts 1:8; 1 Peter 2:9): witnesses who have received and continue to experience his grace. Witnesses who have learned therefore to be what I have come to call "graced" witnesses, or "grace-full" Christians as Philip Yancey put it.[14]

Graced Witnesses

Yancey provides a sweeping but beautiful and biblically-based (e.g., see Eph. 1:6–7; 2:8–9; 1 Peter 5:10) definition of grace in relation to God: "*Grace means there is nothing we can do to make God love us more*—no amount of spiritual calisthenics and renunciations, no amount of knowledge gained from seminaries and divinity schools, no amount of crusading on behalf of righteous causes. *And grace means there is nothing we can do to make God love us less*—no amount of racism or pride or pornography or adultery or even murder. Grace means that God already loves us as much as an infinite God can possibly love."[15] As undeserved but lovingly invited recipients of the amazing grace of God, we can now be graced witnesses or grace-full Christians who reach out and serve others. We will not witness out of superiority and arrogance or pride, thinking and speaking as if we have all the answers to the questions and struggles of those we are reaching out to with the good news of Jesus Christ and his love. When we share the gospel, we will be much more gracious or graced or grace-full, much more vulnerable and humble, much more loving and sacrificial, much more broken—with much more kindness that flows out of a heart full of gratitude for grace so amazing and so divine.

Yancey therefore concludes:

> A grace-full Christian is one who looks at the world through 'grace-tinted lenses' . . . Church should be a haven for people who feel terrible about themselves—theologically, that is our ticket for entry. God needs humble people (which usually means humbled people) to accomplish his work. Whatever makes us feel superior to other people, whatever tempts us to convey a sense of superiority, that is gravity, not grace.[16]

How then do we go about witnessing as graced or grace-full Christians in servant evangelism? We need to rethink and reinvent evangelism or witnessing as we live and serve Jesus in the twenty-first century, looking at the world with grace-tinted lenses from the heart of God: the God of all grace (1 Peter 5:10).

Rethinking and Reinventing Evangelism

A recent issue of *Theology, News, and Notes* (Fall, 2004) focused on "The Challenge of Evangelism in the 21st Century." In a thought-provoking and challenging article, Brian McLaren, a prolific author and leader in the emergent church movement and ministry in the postmodern context, offered five strategies for a radical rethinking of our evangelistic practice:

1. Admit we may not actually understand the good news, and seek to rediscover it (or, Reboot our theology in a new understanding of the gospel of Jesus).
2. (Re)define what a disciple is (or, Change believers into be-alivers and be-lovers).
3. Do good works, including reconciliation with other Christians (or, Recenter the Great Commission in the Great Commandment).
4. Decrease church attendance (or, Deploy Christians into their neighborhoods and communities and world to build relationships with everyone they can, especially the last, the lost, the least).
5. Start new "hives" of Christianity, without blowing up or stirring existing hives (or, Create catholic missional monastic faith communities).[17]

McLaren has issued five radical challenges for how we go about doing evangelism in a world that is becoming more postmodern. Whether we agree with him or have some difference of opinion, we do need as servants of Jesus to engage in evangelism that is servant evangelism at heart: kind evangelism by graced witnesses and grace-full people!

Eddie Gibbs, provided a succinct summary of "*What is the Gospel?*" based on weeks of discussion and preaching on this theme by Fuller faculty members: "The gospel or good news is first and foremost about God and what he has accomplished in Christ Jesus, who inaugurated the reign of God through his incarnation, his dying for our forgiveness and rising that we might become part of God's story of redemption, by being restored to a right relationship with God, adopted into his family, filled with his Spirit, and sent out into the world to continue the ministry of Jesus."[18]

Gibbs then offered the following ten principles for a reinvented evangelism:

> 1. We need to be energized by a fresh realization of the radical and comprehensive nature of the gospel. 2. We must communicate the gospel as the story of God's saving mission in the world rather than as a series of abstract propositions. 3. Our conviction must be that evangelization emerges from the heart of the Church rather than being fabricated at the periphery. 4. We understand that decisions for Christ must express a commitment to be a disciple of Christ. 5. The Church must share the good news in the context of the marketplace of ideas and beliefs . . . *all evangelism has become a cross-cultural activity*. 6. We must assume that God is already at work in a person's life prior to the arrival of any evangelist. 7. We must communicate in a clear, caring, compelling, and compassionate manner. 8. We must invite people to become involved in a community of believers as the first step in believing. 9. We must be open to the possibility that God has something significant to teach through the person(s) with whom we are sharing the good news. 10. We must allow time for people to process both intellectually and emotionally what they have heard and experienced. . . . We must never lose sight of the fact that the Holy Spirit can and does short-circuit procedures and act contrary to our presuppositions and sense of the right order of things.[19]

Gibbs has given us much food for thought and helpful practical guidelines applicable to servant evangelism.

Contemplative Evangelism

I want to refer to one more article in the same issue of *Theology, News, and Notes*, authored by Richard Peace. He wrote on the crucial relationship between evangelism and spiritual formation, and described an approach to evangelism that makes spiritual formation foundational: "contemplative evangelism." In Peace's own words:

> This would be evangelism of the silent rather than the loud proclamation. It would be evangelism of companionship—as both evangelist and seeker reach out to God. It would be evangelism of the retreat and the small group conversation, rather than evangelism of the large meeting and forceful challenge. It would be evangelism of spiritual direction (in which the voice of God is sought) rather than evangelism of the witnessing monologue. What I am suggesting is that by the very act of pursuing spiritual formation via the classical spiritual disciplines, the evangelist will find whole new ways of outreach. This kind of contemplative evangelism resonates with the spiritual pursuits of men and women at the start of the 21st century.[20]

Evangelists need spiritual formation, including the practice of classical spiritual exercises or disciplines, in order to reach out to others.

Contemplative evangelism is not the only valid form of evangelism, but it is an important and underutilized approach to reaching out to others. It is an excellent example of servant evangelism done with kindness and humility.

Prayer Evangelism

In a somewhat different vein, and in the context of spiritual warfare in evangelism, Ed Silvoso wrote about prayer evangelism: "Prayer is the most tangible trace of eternity in the human heart. Intercessory prayer on behalf of the felt needs of the lost is the best way to open their eyes to the light of the gospel."[21] Servant evangelism will therefore include prayer evangelism: the kind and loving act of intercessory prayer for people who do not yet know Jesus personally.

Servant Evangelism—Flexible and Sensitive

Although I have focused much on the need to rethink and reinvent evangelism in today's increasingly postmodern world, I want to note that there are several excellent books available on how to be faithful and fruitful witnesses for Christ, using a variety of different approaches, both more traditional as well as more contemporary, but written mainly from a modern rather than postmodern perspective.[22] Ultimately, the Holy Spirit will lead us, like the apostle Paul, to be all things to all people so that by all means we might save some (1 Cor. 9:22): We will be flexible and sensitive, with kindness and love, in our servant evangelism. We will do "whatever it takes,"[23] as Brad Kallenberg has put it, in full dependence on the Holy Spirit, to reach out to the world in servant evangelism of all kinds, but always with kindness.

The particular style or approach to evangelism that we take will partly depend on our personalities and spiritual gifts. Bill Hybels and Mark Mittelberg, in *Becoming a Contagious Christian*, described six biblical styles of evangelism: Peter's confrontational approach, Paul's intellectual approach, the blind man's testimonial approach, Matthew's interpersonal approach, the Samaritan woman's invitational approach, and Dorcas's service approach.[24] Some of us will be able, with the Holy Spirit's help, to engage in several or all of these styles of evangelism. Hybels and Mittelberg also described a cryptic formula to summarize the basic principles of evangelism that help us to be contagious Christians: HP (a High Potency Christian character) + CP (Close Proximity to our friends) + CC (Clear Communication of the gospel message) = MI (Maximum Impact).[25]

From a more postmodern perspective, McLaren has freshly described evangelism as a dance following the love song of God, as disciple-making, conversation, friendship, influence, an invitation, companionship, challenge, opportunity, and hence as something you get to do. He stresses that you and your friends are more ready for this than you realize! He therefore critiques the following traditional views of evangelism as: sales pitch, conquest, warfare, ultimatum, threat, proof, argument, entertainment, show, monologue, and hence as something you have to do.[26] Again, we don't have to agree with McLaren on every point, but he has challenged us to be radically biblical and culturally relevant and sensitive in our outreach to an increasingly postmodern American society.

To do whatever it takes to reach out to the world, the church today needs to move from a tendency to be inward-focused to truly be outward-focused (like the Antioch church in Acts). Sjogren shared how it took ten years to come up with a mission statement for his church that reflects a commitment to being an outward-focused church with its priority loving those beyond church walls: "We're here to love our city into relationship with Christ."[27] A decade ago, Rick Warren and Bill and Lynne Hybels wrote about being churches that sensitively reach out to seekers and others who do not yet know Christ.[28] To be a truly outward-focused church will eventually mean a church that reaches out in world missions, to the ends of the earth—an Antioch church, as Ross Paterson has pointed out. George Barna has similarly emphasized the need to understand and reach out to the unchurched.[29]

On a Personal Note

I would like to conclude this chapter on servanthood and evangelism, or servant evangelism, by sharing three personal stories of my experiences in witnessing. I believe, by the way, that one of the spiritual gifts God has graciously given me is in this area of evangelism as an evangelist (Eph. 4:11). Ever since my conversion experience in 1968, God has granted me a deep compassion for people, especially for those who do not yet know him. He has also given me freedom and joy in sharing the gospel with others, and quite a number of people have become Christians as a result of our conversations together about Jesus and his love for us.

The first story is about a man I met some years ago at a store in Pasadena, California, while we were both shopping for a stereo sound system. He was from France and was working in Pasadena as a postdoctoral scientist doing research in astronomy. We "bumped" into each other at the store, and he asked me for some advice about the particular product he was planning to buy. While chatting, I sensed, as I prayed in my heart, that this was a divine appointment the Holy Spirit had set up. I therefore invited this man to my small group consisting of a dozen or so members who met twice a month. Since he was new to town, he agreed to come and visit with the small group, and even to visit my church. He wasn't a Christian and had many questions about faith, God, and Christ, initially with many objections to faith coming from his scientific training. Nevertheless, he started attending the small group meeting at my home. And he kept coming back, meeting after meeting, for almost two years!

In our small group meetings, we ate dinner together before having a typical Bible study, ending with a time of open and vulnerable sharing and sincere, loving prayer for one another. He not only attended, he also participated! There were times when some of us Christians were feeling tired and wanted to skip the Bible study. He was the one who objected because he found the Bible fascinating and deeply relevant to his questions and needs! He also shared openly and vulnerably, and often asked for prayer even though he had not yet accepted Christ and wasn't sure about the existence of God. Over the two years, we became good friends and had many deep discussions and spiritual conversations. He then returned to France because his postdoctoral research stint in

Pasadena had been completed. He told me and the small group that when he first came to join us he did not believe in God, just like many of his friends who were scientists, physicists, or astronomers. At the time of his return to France, he had come a long way in his faith journey, and said he now believed there is a God—he even tried to convince his scientific colleagues of the existence of God, but they ended up laughing at him, a fellow scientist! However, he was still not sure about Jesus as Lord and Savior, and was not ready to accept Christ, although I had shared the gospel with him several times.

Two years later, after my friend had gone back to France to work, he came to Southern California to attend a conference. We met again in my office at Fuller Seminary and had a good chat. This time, after I briefly shared the gospel once more, he said he had no more reasons for not accepting Christ. So right there in my office, we prayed together, and he asked Jesus into his heart to be his Lord and Savior—and best friend! I share this story because it illustrates, from real life, that when we reach out to people with sincere kindness and love, and develop spiritual friendships with them, God is working. This kind of servant evangelism involves opening our lives and homes to them, letting them see our own struggles and needs as fellow pilgrims on the faith journey, and caring for them, even praying for them *before* they decide to accept Christ, over a period of time that can stretch to years. When we do so, God is working—and working—to touch them deeply. Some of them will become Christians, like this French scientist friend of mine. I have learned over thirty-seven years as a Christian that evangelism has to be real and authentic to effectively touch people for Christ! Ultimately, it doesn't matter what method or style or approach we take in our evangelistic outreach. What matters is that it is real and authentic, filled with love and kindness in a servant evangelism that comes straight from the heart of Jesus and his passion and compassion for the lost, and that is anointed by the presence and power of the Holy Spirit.

My second story is similar. It has to do with witnessing to a young man who was in law school when we first started talking together about Jesus, usually over lunch, a few years ago. I would often buy lunch for him and we had several good spiritual conversations. He was dating a Christian woman from my church. They were engaged to be married fourteen months later in November 2004. They wanted me to perform their wedding, but they both were concerned that he was not yet a Christian. I met with him for lunch again several times, occasionally with his fiancée, but more often with him alone. He had many questions and doubts about the Christian faith, and we honestly grappled with them in our discussions. By this time he had already graduated from law school.

As a bright young man, he asked many sharp and good questions. I shared with him as many answers as I could, based on the Bible and Christian apologetics, but I also honestly admitted I did not have answers to all of his searching questions. I presented a range of options possible within the spectrum of Christian belief, in response to some of his questions on topics such as abortion, homosexuality, creation versus evolution, heaven and hell, the inspiration of Scripture, the existence of God, and the uniqueness of Jesus Christ. In my earlier years as a younger and less mature Christian, I would have tried to give absolute dogmatic answers to all of his questions. I have learned over the years to be more humble, more authentic, and more vulnerable in my spiritual conversations with people—and to really love them with the compassion of Jesus. I have learned from our conversations as well, as we journey together on this pilgrimage of faith. However, when the Bible clearly gives an answer, I did not and still do not compromise on what I truly believe to be the God-inspired biblical answers!

We did not just discuss issues of faith when I met with this young man. Servant evangelism includes acts of love plus words of love plus adequate time. We also talked about his life and future, including his career options as a law graduate and his upcoming marriage. I listened as deeply and sensitively as I could, with the Holy Spirit's help, giving feedback when appropriate. I also offered to pray for him and his needs, an offer which he always accepted. But he was still not ready to receive Christ personally and become his disciple. I continued to pray for him daily, and to meet with him for lunch every few weeks. His fiancée and others were praying for him, too, and doing their part in ministering to him. About three months before his wedding date, we met again for lunch. This time, before I could even ask him where he stood with Christ, he told me that he felt he was ready to make a commitment, to accept Jesus into his heart and life as his Lord and Savior. I almost fell off my chair at the restaurant, overjoyed at what he had just said! I, together with his fiancée and her Christian family members and friends, had been prayerfully waiting not just months, but years for this special moment of grace to happen! He said he felt ready not because I had answered all his questions—he still had some doubts and unanswered, lingering questions about the Christian faith. However, he was satisfied with many of the answers I had provided and deeply appreciated my honest answers and lack of answers when there were none. Most of all, he expressed being deeply touched that I did not pressure or buttonhole him into accepting Christ, but gave him the space and time he needed to really think through the issues. I was humbled to hear him say that he had decided that day to accept Christ because of me more than my answers, because of the love and kindness he experienced in our times together. I wept inside. This was obviously a God thing! It was not about me, but about God in me and through me. What a privilege to be God's servant in servant evangelism, in one of the most joyful experiences we can have on earth—leading someone to Christ!

We ended up driving back to my office because it was close to the restaurant where we had lunch that day. There, after briefly going over the gospel again, he prayed to receive Christ as his Lord and Savior. He had tears, and so did I. It was a deeply moving experience for both of us. Several weeks later, after meeting him and his fiancée for premarital preparation sessions and follow-up of his decision, I had the blessed privilege of conducting their wedding in November 2004. It was a beautiful wedding, blessed by God, with sunshine despite weather forecasts of rain! We had experienced genuine servant evangelism with a huge dose of love and kindness, authenticity and awe because of the amazing and matchless grace and love of God he has shown us in Christ. We love people because we truly love God, but always because he first loved us and continues to love us (1 John 4:19).

Let me close with one final story. I fly several times a year to attend or speak at various conferences and meetings here and abroad. I always pray beforehand that I be sensitive to the Holy Spirit's leading in possible divine appointments to share Jesus with someone on board, usually the person sitting next to me. A few years ago, I met an older woman who was flying home from visiting her adult daughter suffering from health problems. As is my usual custom, I had with me a copy of Bill Bright's "The Four Spiritual Laws" published by Campus Crusade for Christ. I shared it with her after we had a long conversation in which she told me her struggles and emotional pain over her daughter's physical condition. (People often open up and tell me all kinds of things when they find out that I am a psychologist as well as a pastor!) I gave a copy of the Four Laws to her, and we took a break from talking. While taking a short nap, I suddenly awoke and saw her crying as she read the pamphlet. I gently asked her if she was okay, and she said she was crying with tears of joy over the beautiful truths she had been reading, and especially the prayer for accepting Christ as Lord and Savior. I asked her if she had ever prayed that prayer before. Although she came from a religious church background, she had not. When I further asked her if she would like to pray that prayer with me, she immediately and gladly said, "Yes." We prayed together, right there on that plane, and she asked Jesus into her heart. This is an example of a traditional, up front approach to evangelism where there was not time to develop a spiritual friendship over weeks, months, or even years. I had a few hours on the plane, and she was ready—because God had already been working in her heart before we met on the plane that day. But it was a few hours filled with the love of God and compassion of Jesus for a woman in deep emotional pain and spiritual need and longing. Servant evangelism is sensitive to meeting such needs directly and immediately when and if the Spirit leads. We need to remember that some of the old, traditional ways of sharing our faith are still good. Richard Mouw, president of Fuller Theological Seminary, has written: "This is also what I want for the evangelical movement: a mature discovery of what was good about the sawdust trail."[30]

Bill Hybels and Mark Mittelberg have emphasized: "People matter to God!"[31] People matter deeply to God, and they are most precious to him. He loves every one of us, "not wanting anyone to perish, but everyone to come to repentance" (2 Peter 3:9). He wants all people to be saved and to come to a knowledge of the truth in Christ (1 Tim. 2:3–4). He has therefore called us, as his servants, to be involved in servant evangelism, in "whatever it takes" with deep kindness and authentic love, to bring people to Christ, even to the ends of the earth. This is his heartbeat, his priority. It should be ours as well! Hybels and Mittelberg therefore challenge us: "There's nothing like the adventure of being used by God to contagiously spread His love, truth, and life to other people—people who matter deeply to Him. So let's get on with it!"[32] It is the most loving act we can do for others, as Billy Graham has put it: "I am convinced that the greatest act of love we can ever perform for people is to tell them about God's love for them in Christ."[33]

In telling people about God's love for them in Christ, servants of Jesus in servant evangelism also *show* people God's love by acts of kindness. And sometimes God will call and lead us to do not just little things or small things with great love, but big things or "great" things with great love, as he recently moved Bruce Wilkinson to do in Africa. Wilkinson, in *The Dream Giver*,[34] has told stories of how God has worked miraculously in different parts of Africa in significant ways to deal with hunger, orphans, poverty, and the tragic AIDS epidemic. Servant evangelism includes doing whatever God wants—whether small or big things, but always with great love, his love—to *show* people his love in Christ. World missions, or outreach to the ends of the earth, will also include social concern and social action with justice and mercy, or "Kingdom Ethics" as Glen Stassen and David Gushee have put it.[35] Servants of Jesus Christ will not just tell about God's love, they will show it. This is the real show and tell of the gospel of Jesus Christ by his true servants in servant evangelism that is kindness fully blossomed and manifested as part of the fruit of the Holy Spirit. It's a God thing!

11

Servanthood in the Church

Beginning with this chapter, we will cover servanthood in specific areas of our lives and ministries: the church, the home, and the workplace and school. Servanthood in the church is a crucial topic for us to consider in more detail in this chapter. We have already seen how God called us to be not only servants of Christ (1 Cor. 4:1) but also servants of those we are ministering to, especially in the church context (2 Cor. 4:5). Paul asserts in 1 Corinthians 3:5–7, 9: "What, after all, is Apollos? And what is Paul? Only servants, through whom you came to believe—as the Lord has assigned to each his task. I planted the seed, Apollos watered it, but God made it grow. So neither he who plants nor he who waters is anything, but only God, who makes things grow. . . . For we are God's fellow workers; you are God's field, God's building." The Lord has given us spiritual gifts to use in apostolic, prophetic, evangelistic, pastoral, and teaching ministries in the church in order "to prepare God's people for works of service, so that the body of Christ may be built up until we all reach unity in the faith and in the knowledge of the Son of God and become mature, attaining to the whole measure of the fullness of Christ" (Eph. 4:12–13). Maturity in Christ is the ultimate goal of ministry in the church and beyond.

Growing Up into Maturity in Christ

John Stott, in his opening address at the First International Consultation on Discipleship held in September 1999 on England's scenic south coast, said:

> I wonder how you would sum up the Christian situation in the world today. For me, it's a strange, rather tragic, and disturbing paradox. On the one hand, in many parts of the world the church is growing by leaps and bounds. But on the other hand, throughout the church, superficiality is everywhere. That's the paradox. Growth without depth.
>
> No doubt God is not pleased with superficial discipleship. The apostolic writers of the New Testament declare with one voice that God wants His people to grow up and to grow into maturity in Christ. . . . Where then shall we find the authentic Jesus so that we may grow in our understanding of Him and in our relationship with Him? The answer, of course, is in the Scriptures. Scripture is God's portrait of His Son, painted by the Holy Spirit. . . . If only the veil could be taken away from our eyes, if only we could see Jesus in the fullness of His divine human person and His saving work, then we would see that He's worthy of our complete allegiance, our love, and our worship. Nothing is more important.[1]

These are powerful and challenging words that the church today, here and abroad, needs to heed. As servants of Jesus in the church, we will be involved not only in servant evangelism and servant warfare, but also in disciple-making, being devoted disciples ourselves, and serving in various ministries to present everyone mature in Christ.

The Present State of the Church

George Barna, well-known church pollster and researcher, has recently lamented the sad and sorry state of the church in America today. A few years ago, he urgently challenged Christians to grow in spiritual maturity and the church to be the true representation of Christ by serving God and humanity. Barna described the situation of today's church as urgent but not hopeless. He emphasized that time is of the essence, and we need to respond soon.[2]

More recently, Barna expressed feeling even more discouraged about the future of the church, believing that his ten-year campaign to reform the church had failed. In an article in *Christianity Today*,[3] Tim Stafford noted that Barna had issued a dramatic ultimatum in 1998, that we only had about five years for the church in America to turn around and really begin to affect the culture rather than vice-versa. Barna, in 2002, pessimistically answered, "Nothing's changing, and the change that we see is not for the better."[4] Barna is convinced that the majority of pastors and church workers today are not leaders and do not have the gift of leadership that is so desperately needed by the church. He hopes to develop a new generation of leaders, starting as early as high school, so that in twenty or thirty years' time, there will be a healthy, dynamic church.[5]

Barna's main hope therefore to turn the church around is still to develop leaders with the leadership gift who can formulate clearly God's vision for the church and the world, communicate it effectively, and mobilize and motivate church members to follow such a vision in obedience to God's leading. His analysis can be criticized for being based too much on an entrepreneurial model of the church, requiring a certain kind of CEO leadership. His approach is similar to Bill Hybel's emphasis on the need for courageous leadership in the church because leaders are supposedly the hope of the church. However, we have already seen in earlier chapters of this book that it would be more accurate to say that servants are the hope of the church, including the servants who may have been called and gifted by God to lead: leading servants, or servant leaders so-called, with a servant heart who serve by leading.

The crucial need for true servanthood in the church today cannot be overemphasized, precisely because such a high premium has been put on a certain kind of strong, visionary leadership to change the church and turn it around. There is a certain danger to such an emphasis on strong leadership: It may not be founded on true servanthood and devoted discipleship that follows Jesus all the way. Strong leadership of the wrong kind, often based on secular CEO and business management models, can end up with much pride, self-sufficiency, and therefore sin. What the church needs in order to be transformed into an Acts 2 type of community of faith (Acts 2:42–47) is the presence of true servants of Jesus who are filled with the Spirit, manifesting his fruit of love, joy, peace, patience, kindness, goodness, faithfulness, gentleness, and self-control (Gal. 5:22–23). The church needs servants who engage in true service rather than self-righteous service and who will lead when called by God to do so, with humility and grace, in prayerful consultation with a plurality of other fellow servants also called to lead, in order to have a vision for the church that is God's, and not a vision born of human ambition or wanting to be great or to do great things.

Living Like Jesus in the Church

Ronald Sider, who teaches at Eastern Seminary and serves as president of Evangelicals for Social Action, has described Christian faith as servanthood and emphasized the need for servanthood in every area of our lives, especially for leaders in the church. He wrote: "Genuine Christians embrace servanthood. . . . Nothing is more important today than for Christians to recover genuine servanthood. . . . What would happen if the church today recovered Jesus' pattern of humble service? . . . The answer is clear: The world would stop to watch—and be changed. . . . Christianity as servanthood could transform our homes and our nations. But that will never happen unless the church's leaders truly become servants. . . . The more faithfully Christians follow the Servant King, the more our evangelism will have power, our marriages will have wholeness, and our societies will enjoy justice."[6]

In living like Jesus in the church as true servants, we do not necessarily try to imitate him: we follow him by living in him in intimate, loving friendship. Living like Jesus means living *in* Jesus first! As we do that, abiding in him, he will produce spiritual fruit in us and form us to become more and more like him (John 15:5).

Developing a Biblical Worldview

Living like Jesus also means we will be thinking like Jesus as we get to know him and his Word, the Bible. Barna has reported the alarming statistics that about 91 percent of all born-again adults do not have a biblical worldview, and around 98 percent of all born-again teenagers do not have a biblical worldview! These statistics of course may not apply or be true for a particular church. We have just completed a similar survey of close to 200 young people and adults in the church I am pastoring, and we are glad to see a significant majority of the people surveyed subscribing to a biblical worldview. A biblical worldview was basically defined by Barna as consisting of at least the following six central biblical beliefs: "God is the all-knowing, all-powerful, Creator of the universe who still rules that universe today; When Jesus Christ was on earth He lived a sinless life; Satan is not just a symbol of evil but is a real, living entity; A person cannot earn his or her eternal salvation by being good or doing good things for other people, that salvation is the free gift of God; Every person who believes in Jesus Christ has a personal responsibility to share his or her faith in Him with other people who believe differently; and The Bible is totally accurate in all that it teaches."[7]

Barna has described some practical ways in which a church can systematically help its members to develop a biblical worldview and think more like Jesus, including doing so early with children and young people.[8] The crucial foundation of thinking like Jesus and having a biblical worldview is of course to really know the Bible well, and to apply the eternal truths of Scripture to our daily lives and ministries as servants of Christ. Ajith Fernando calls this being "saturated in the Word," which includes regular, deep Bible study and the use of Scriptures in our teaching and preaching and other ministries.[9] Stott, as we saw earlier, has also emphasized the need to get deep into Scripture if we are to really know the authentic Jesus and grow mature in him. While God's Word is thus central, it is part of a broader framework of spiritual formation or growing to maturity in Christ that should be the ultimate goal of church life together.

Spiritual Formation in the Local Church

Dallas Willard, in *Renovation of the Heart*, included a chapter on spiritual formation in the local congregation. He emphasized that the right direction to take is to make "spiritual formation in Christlikeness *the exclusive primary goal of the local congregation*."[10] In doing so, we must guard especially against what he calls "simple *distraction*" which characterizes so many local congregations or churches today: getting distracted with the minor, secondary aspects of church life such as buildings, worship styles, rules for Sunday school, times and numbers of church meetings, and so forth. Willard quotes Leith Anderson who pointed out that the New Testament is actually silent about many matters or details that we associate with church life and structure, although it speaks often about churches in terms of principles and biblical absolutes. The details can be real and dangerous distractions (if they take much or all of our time) from the primary and exclusive goal of any local church or congregation: spiritual formation in Christlikeness.[11]

Willard provides helpful material on how we as servants in the church can pursue the primary and exclusive goal of the local church: maturity in Christ or spiritual formation in Christlikeness. This goal impacts and transforms every area of our being: the mind, will (heart or spirit) and character, body, social dimension, and soul. The general and reliable pattern for such transformation into Christlikeness can be summarized in an acronym "VIM": *V*ision of life in the kingdom of God (referring to the range of God's effective will, where what God wants done is done) now and forever, *I*ntention to be a kingdom person (we can and need to *decide* to live life in the kingdom, fully relying on Jesus and *intending* to obey him), and *M*eans of spiritual transformation into Christlikeness and maturity in Christ, which include the practice of spiritual disciplines.[12]

Based on Matthew 28:18–20 as God's plan for the blessing and growth of local congregations as well as for the church in general, Willard suggests three stages of such a plan for spiritual formation in the local congregation: "1. Making disciples—that is apprentices of Jesus. 2. Immersing the apprentices at all levels of growth in the Trinitarian presence. 3. Transforming disciples inwardly, in such a way that doing the words and deeds of Christ is not the focus but is the natural outcome or side effect."[13] As we live in Jesus and follow him as his servants in the church, we will help others in all the various ways in which he may call us to serve, to similarly know and follow Jesus.

Willard concludes with this challenge as well as encouragement to the church to focus on its primary goal of spiritual formation in Christlikeness: "No special talents, personal skills, educational programs, money, or possessions are required to bring this to pass. We do not have to purify and enforce some legalistic system. Just ordinary people who are apprentices, gathered in the name of Jesus and immersed in his presence, and taking steps of inward transformation as they put on the character of Christ: this is all that is required. . . . Let that be our only aim, and the triumph of God in our individual lives and our times is ensured. The renovation of the heart, putting on the character of Christ, is the unfailing key. It will provide for human life all the blessing that money, talent, education, and good fortune in this world cannot begin to supply, and will strongly anticipate, within this present life, a glorious entry into the full presence of God."[14]

Church Health

In *The Purpose-Driven Church*, Rick Warren described how to grow a church without compromising your message and mission. He emphasized church health first, by focusing on balancing the five major New Testament purposes of any church, based on the Great Commandment (Matt. 22:37–40) and the Great Commission (Matt. 28:19–20): worship, ministry (service), evangelism, fellowship, and discipleship. The church therefore exists to "*edify, encourage, exalt, equip, and evangelize*."[15] Warren then provided the following purpose statement of Saddleback Church where he serves as senior pastor, which incorporates all five purposes: "To bring people to Jesus and *membership* in his family, to develop them into Christlike *maturity*, and equip them for their *ministry* in the church and life *mission* in the world in order to *magnify* God's name."[16] He asserts that healthy, lasting church growth must be balanced and multidimensional, with five balanced facets or purposes: "Every church needs to grow *warmer* through fellowship, *deeper* through discipleship, *stronger* through worship, *broader* through ministry, and *larger* through evangelism."[17]

Servanthood in the church will mean keeping these five New Testament purposes in view and in balance, so that the church will become a healthy, biblically-based church as God's people or community of faith in Christ. It will also mean that the church will consist of devoted disciples of Christ who walk the way of servanthood: everyone serving Jesus, and as He leads us, serving one another and the world. We therefore need to return the ministry to the people of God and not restrict it only to ordained clergy or church leaders, as Greg Ogden has so well challenged us to do.[18] We will then experience purpose-driven lives in purpose-driven churches. I prefer to talk about purpose-deepened or purpose-directed lives and churches, empowered by the Holy Spirit, rather than "driven." There is already too much drivenness or activism in many of our lives and churches. However, since Rick Warren is for healthy churches, not driven, stressed-out or burned out churches, by purpose-driven he actually means purpose-motivated, or what I have called purpose-deepened or purpose-directed.

With regard to church health, Stephen Macchia has offered the following ten characteristics of a healthy church: (1) God's empowering presence; (2) God-exalting worship; (3) spiritual disciplines; (4) learning and growing in community; (5) a commitment to loving and caring relationships; (6) servant-leadership development; (7) an outward focus; (8) wise administration and accountability; (9) networking with the body of Christ; and (10) stewardship and generosity.[19]

In a similar vein, but focusing more specifically on the emotionally healthy church and a strategy for discipleship that actually changes lives, Peter Scazzero pointed out the missing link in discipleship: the link between emotional health and spiritual maturity. Sharing vulnerably from his own experiences of emotional pain, he emphasized that in church life and ministry, "as go the leaders, so go the church."[20] He then described six helpful principles of an emotionally healthy church: "(1) look beneath the surface; (2) break the power of the past; (3) live in brokenness and vulnerability; (4) receive the gift of limits; (5) embrace grieving and loss; and (6) make incarnation your model for loving well."[21]

Servants in the church will apply such principles in their service and ministry to build an emotionally healthy church.

God's Intent for the Church

We have already covered Warren's five major New Testament purposes for every purpose-driven church. Another way of looking at church and how to be servants of Jesus in the church is to rediscover or reclaim God's original intent for the church. Wes Roberts and Glenn Marshall have recently done just this in their book, *Reclaiming God's Original Intent for the Church*. They focused on: the much older ways, authenticity, making disciples, calling, character, community, trusting God, following the Spirit, servanthood, fruit, listening, love, and our Triune God.[22]

Servants will minister in the church in ways that will fulfill God's original intent for the church as Roberts and Marshall have so clearly explicated. It's about loving service and helping the church to be a caring church, including lay caregiving and lay counseling or servant counseling,[23] fully dependent on God, and full of God and his grace and presence so that people can be built up in the body of Christ and become more mature in Christlikeness, in wholeness and holiness, in agape love.

Pastoral Ministry and Leadership

Much has been written and discussed about what pastoral ministry and especially pastoral leadership in the church should look like. There has been an emphasis, as pointed out earlier, on strong, visionary leadership in the church, whether from the pastor or senior pastor, or other lay leaders in the congregation. This emphasis is based on a CEO model of pastoral and church leadership that is gaining more widespread influence in today's church, which is increasingly being viewed as an organization rather than a living organism in Christ. I believe that such an emphasis is potentially dangerous if an even stronger emphasis on servanthood in leaders is not made as often, if not more often. As Sider has asserted: "Christianity as servanthood could transform our homes and nations. But that will never happen unless the church's leaders truly become servants."[24] Pastoral leadership and church leadership in general must be characterized and marked by true servanthood. Otherwise, there is no hope for the church! The hope of the church is in true servanthood that is Christ-centered and Christlike.

Sider goes on to say: "As Christ looks on the contemporary church, he sees church leaders who abuse power, live extravagantly, and jockey for fame and prestige. He must weep. . . . Thank God that is not the total picture. There are scores of unknown servant leaders scattered through the church. . . . Biblical ethical standards are what our crazy society longs for, even without knowing it. But they will never be able to hear our message unless we share it as servants."[25]

In describing Christian faith as basically servanthood, and therefore genuine Christians embrace servanthood, Sider provides ten other essential characteristics of genuine Christians who are true servants. Genuine Christians "embrace both God's holiness and God's love, live like Jesus, keep their marriage covenants and put children before career, nurture daily spiritual renewal and live in the power of the Holy Spirit, strive to make the church a little picture of what heaven will be like, love the whole person the way Jesus did, mourn church divisions and embrace all who confess Jesus as God and Savior, confess that Jesus is Lord of politics and economics, share God's special concern for the poor, treasure the creation and worship the Creator."[26]

David Fisher, in his vision and description of the twenty-first century pastor, pointed out that pastoral integrity is cultivated by pastors learning to be servants and stewards, so that they do not abuse the power they have. Fisher wrote: "Power provides a great capacity for corruption. Pastoral life is about power. Pastors have organizational power, personal power, spiritual power, pulpit power, and financial power—the power of trust and office and souls. Abuse of power is as basic an evil as there is, and it lies at the heart of pastoral and ecclesial failure. The antidote is the foundational Christian value of submission."[27] Strong, visionary, powerful church leadership must be tempered with the heart of servanthood, full of brokenness, humility, submission, and loving service. The Holy Spirit will produce such fruit in us as we submit to the lordship of Christ as true servants who have also been called by God to lead.

It is encouraging to note that in recent years a growing number of books have been written emphasizing that pastoral ministry and leadership should not primarily follow the secular CEO or entrepreneurial business models. Instead, more biblical models of pastors as primarily spiritual shepherds of God's people or flock have been advocated or reclaimed, and rightly so![28] As such, criteria for spiritual maturity as explicated in biblical texts such as 1 Timothy 3:1–12 and Titus 1:5–9 are crucial for choosing church leaders and pastors.[29] The need to be faithful and countercultural servants of the gospel and hence to be "unnecessary" pastors (unnecessary according to the world's criteria, which focus on false expectations or goals of charisma and success, numbers, and power), has also been emphasized, especially by Marva Dawn and Eugene Peterson.[30]

Simon Chan, in *Spiritual Theology*, clearly described the distinguishing mark of the pastoral vocation or ministry: "In the modern church, the role of the pastor is no longer clear-cut. The pastor is expected to do a lot of things but is not sure which is 'the one thing needful' (Luke 10:42), the essential duty. The recovery of spiritual direction in recent years has once again drawn attention to the main focus of pastoral care, namely, to help Christians develop their prayer life and discover the will of God. For much of the history of the church, the work of the pastor was quite unambiguous: the 'cure of souls'. The shepherd is to help the sheep assimilate and live out the spiritual life. In short, the pastor is essentially a spiritual theologian and a guide to godliness. It is this work and nothing else that gives the pastoral vocation its distinguishing mark."[31]

Unfortunately, there may be many congregations or churches that want a very different kind of pastor than the biblically-based, historical description just provided of the pastor as shepherd, spiritual theologian, and guide. Eugene Peterson has some strong words to say about this: "And we are unnecessary to what *congregations* insist that we must do and be: as the experts who help them stay ahead of the competition. . . . They want pastors who *lead*. . . . Congregations get their ideas of what makes a pastor from the culture, not from the Scriptures: they want a winner; they want their needs met; they want to be part of something zesty and glamorous. . . . With hardly an exception they don't want pastors at all—they want managers of their religious company. They want a pastor they can follow so they won't have to bother with following Jesus anymore."[32]

In a similar vein, Leith Anderson exposes four myths or false ideas about leadership, especially in the church, that must be given up: Leaders must have all the right traits; leadership is all about leaders; all leaders are heroes; and pastors must have the gift of leadership. He concludes that leadership really has to do simply with figuring out what needs to be done and then doing it.[33] Pastors then are shepherds or spiritual guides and servants first to the flock of God in the church. Pastoral or church leadership when exercised is done in the spirit of servanthood. The exclusive primary goal again is the spiritual formation of the congregation into mature Christlikeness.

Servanthood in pastoral ministry and leadership in the church means learning to serve as true shepherds—with love. Roberts and Marshall put it this way: "True shepherds understand what it means to have a shepherd's heart. True shepherds know their sheep and are more concerned about the sheep than saving their own skin. True shepherds are willing to bear the scars, the disappointments, and the hardships of the task because they care deeply for their sheep. One thing is true if we're going to shepherd our flocks like Jesus: It's about love."[34]

The Need for More Followers

The need for more and better, often defined as stronger leadership in the church, has been sounded over and over again. It is therefore interesting and refreshingly rare to find someone like Leith Anderson, a well-known pastor himself, asking the question, "Do we really need more leaders? Or more followers?" His answer is surprising but right on target! He says in his insightful book: "The Bible says comparatively little about leadership and a great deal about followership. . . . The whole meaning of being a Christian is wrapped up in being a disciple, and being a disciple means being a follower. . . . The twenty-first century church needs some first-rate followers. Perhaps we need good followers more than we need good leaders. . . . It takes only a few leaders to fulfill God's goals. But it takes many followers. . . . For the church of the twenty-first century to be the church God wants it to be will require large numbers of wise, prioritizing, loyal, and supportive followers. Great leaders aren't born, they are made—by great followers."[35]

Servants of Jesus can make significant contributions to the church by serving in various ministries as wise, prioritizing, loyal, and supportive followers, which are needed in large numbers by every and any church! Servants can also serve as leaders when and if God calls them to move into leadership in the church for his kingdom's sake, but always with a servant attitude or heart.

I recently read a thank-you card entitled "With Appreciation for Your Ministry" (Dayspring Cards) that had the following beautiful lines by Roy Lessin: "The beautiful thing about a servant of the Lord is that God gives him the heart of a shepherd. It is a heart that leads instead of a heart that controls; it is a heart that gives instead of a heart that takes; it is a heart that serves instead of a heart that demands; it is a heart that restores instead of a heart that scatters. It is a good heart—it is the only kind of heart that the sheep will follow."

Servants, including pastors and other church leaders, need to have a shepherd's heart like that of Jesus, the Good Shepherd (John 10:11, 14), as we walk daily with him and in him. In caring for the sheep, or God's people, and reaching out to others (John 10:16), having a shepherd's heart will also mean being sensitive to the changing needs of the world, and being flexible in how we minister to people in a culturally relevant way. We do this without compromising the message of the gospel, although the means and methods may need to be adapted. I have covered this point in some detail in the previous chapter focusing on servant evangelism. Servants therefore need to keep up with the latest trends and quantum changes in the culture as well as in the church.[36] This includes learning about the emerging church in North America that is doing ministry in more radical, postmodern ways focusing on mystery and wonder rather than the so-called modern values of objectivity, analysis, and control.[37] It also means learning about the new apostolic churches and what Peter Wagner has described as the coming of the second apostolic age. Whether or not we agree with some of the theology and practice of such contemporary and oftentimes charismatic churches, they are growing by leaps and bounds throughout the world, impacting hundreds of thousands of people.[38]

A Concluding Story

Let me end this chapter on servanthood in the church by sharing a real life story written by Amy Sheng from the First Evangelical Church Association (FECA) of which my church is a founding member. Dr. Chi-Hok Wong, president of FECA and a close friend of mine, helped shape the balanced mission of FECA as: "A joint and integrative ministry of spirituality, mission, and social concern." Spirituality refers to God's longing heart to have communion with his children; mission to God's restless heart for the lost, and social concern to God's compassionate heart for the poor, broken, and oppressed. Amy served as a field worker at First Evangelical Church of St. Petersburg, Russia, a member church of FECA consisting mainly of students. She writes:

> What kind of short-term missions teams bring true blessings to the local missionaries and their ministries? It is those whose motive is only to bring glory to God and those who are willing to serve others wholeheartedly as servants. Their motive is not for "a good report" to bring home. They do not serve to please others. They do not have the pride of being pastors or elders, but see themselves as servants. They come only to serve the local church. They do not ask what others could do for them, but only ask what they could do for the church and how they could become blessings, not burdens, to them. . . . A pastor from one of the FECA member churches has served among the students several times. Each time he had to pay some kind of personal sacrifice in order to make the trip. He is very welcomed by the students! They love to be with him because he always puts the needs of the students before his own. Whenever he comes, he does not ask anything from the church. Instead, he accepts all the arrangements made by the church. Though he does not speak the local language and is not familiar with the surroundings, he always tries to find his own way around without bothering the students. And when the church needs him, he gives his all. He has earned the love and respect from the students. If we could have more of this kind of God's servant among us who takes the attitude and nature of a servant in serving others, and who influences life with his own life, the young Christians would also have the same kind of spiritual life in following and serving the Lord.[39]

I am deeply touched and blessed by such an example of servanthood in the church and in missions in one of my fellow pastors and colleagues of FECA. When church leaders and pastors truly become servants like this pastor, Christianity as servanthood can transform our homes and nations. May we servants of Jesus serve the church with love, and love his church here and abroad.

12

Servanthood in the Home

Servanthood in the home—whether in the marital relationship between husband and wife or in family relationships such as between parents and children and between siblings—is a fundamental and basic area of true servanthood. When Jesus commands us to love our neighbor as ourselves (Mark 12:31), he includes loving our closest neighbor—our spouse, our children, our parents, our siblings—in the home. We often forget that loving our neighbor includes loving our family members: Servanthood begins in the home!

Servanthood in Marriage

Very few couples enter into marriage with the thought of making servanthood in marriage a key priority of their lives together. Many couples, including Christian couples, do not even think of servanthood at all in marriage! In fact, in contemporary, if not postmodern, society, couples tend to be very sensitive to any hint of the need to be submissive or to serve each other. The emphasis in recent years has been much more on how to enrich one's life through marriage. There has therefore been a tendency to focus on what one can get out of marriage, even out of one's spouse, rather than on what one can give to one's spouse, or what one can contribute to marriage. When conducting premarital preparation or counseling sessions, I quite frequently come across couples who believe that marriage is a 50–50 proposition: Each spouse is 50 percent responsible for the marriage. I often have to help such couples see that this is an erroneous, unrealistic, and unbiblical view of marriage. Instead, I try to help them see that marriage is a 100–100 proposition, and even 100–0 if necessary! Each spouse is 100 percent responsible and committed to loving the other, *regardless* of the other's response or lack thereof. This takes deep maturity on the part of each spouse. It also requires servanthood of the most genuine and loving kind—true servanthood in Christ—to make marriage really work. Serving each other, as each other's best friend in the marital relationship, founded on a relationship with our ultimate best friend Jesus Christ, is what marriage that will survive and even thrive is all about! Servanthood in marriage is a crucial part of servanthood in the home, which is basic and fundamental in true servanthood in Christ.

While many books have been written on how to have a fulfilling and enriching marriage, including some good ones from a Christian perspective,[1] there are fewer books with a focus on servanthood as a crucial aspect of marriage, and especially Christian marriage.[2] I will now review some helpful guidelines or suggestions for servanthood—including mutual submission and sacrifice in the context of loving commitment—in marriage.

Mutual Submission

True servants of Jesus who are married understand clearly what Ephesians 5:21–33 really teaches about the roles of husband and wife in biblical marriage. They do not have to fight or argue over what respectful submission to the husband means for the wife, and what sacrificial and nurturing love for the wife means to the husband. They are already servants or bondslaves of Jesus Christ: they understand that Christian marriage means they will be loving and humble servants to each other, as husband and wife in mutual submission, because each of them is first submissive or surrendered to Christ (Eph. 5:21). They realize that mutual submission to each other out of reverence for Christ in Ephesians 5:21 precedes the rest of the text that speaks of wives submitting to and respecting husbands, and husbands loving their wives even to death, just as Christ loved the church and gave himself up and died for the church!

Paul Stevens insightfully points out that mutual submission is actually reversing the curse that came after Adam and Eve fell into sin (Gen. 3:16).

> Rule and revolt is not what God wants between the sexes, but the inevitable consequence of separation from God. But in Christ, instead of *ruling* his wife, the husband *loves* her to death. Instead of revolting against her domestic master, the wife is free to bombard him with respect. This is not what each deserves. It is not even the duty each has to the other. It is gospel freedom, sheer grace. . . . The key to understanding the marriage section of Ephesians 5 is the emphasis on Christ. We submit to one another, Paul says, "out of reverence for Christ" (v. 21). . . . All of these relationships—mutual submission, servant headship and reverence—are *in Christ*. They are not roles but expressions of spirituality. Our life together in Christ is not based simply on mutual submission or on a male-female hierarchy, but on Christ who chooses to dwell in the covenant.[3]

Servants of Christ who are married know that they are married in Christ, and need the continual filling of the Holy Spirit (Eph. 5:18) with his presence and power, to be such loving servants to each other as husband and wife. They become "intimate allies" in the battle against the chaos of life in this world as Dan Allender and Tremper Longman have put it.[4]

Gary Thomas has written what I believe to be one of the best and deepest books on what marriage is really all about from a biblical perspective. He asks the searching question: "What if God designed marriage to make us holy more than to make us happy?" He writes not about how to have a happier or more fulfilling marriage, but about the real purpose of marriage as *sacred* marriage: a spiritual discipline that helps us to know God better, trust him more fully, and love him more deeply. Hence, marriage is not as much about you and your spouse as it is about you and God! In Thomas's own words: "Marriage calls us to an entirely new and selfless life. . . . Any situation that calls me to confront my selfishness has enormous spiritual value, and I slowly began to understand that the real purpose of marriage may not be happiness as much as it is holiness. . . . If we view the marriage relationship as an opportunity to excel in love, it doesn't matter how difficult the person is whom we are called to love; it doesn't matter even whether that love is ever returned. We can still excel at love. We can still say, 'Like it or not, I'm going to love you like nobody ever has.' . . . But there's another challenge when two believers are both committed to pursuing a deeper spiritual reality in marriage—the formidable task of working to become not just a holy spouse, but a holy couple."[5]

Some examples of ways in which we can grow to become more like Christ in sacred marriage include learning to love and respect others, fostering good prayer, having our sin exposed, growing in the spiritual discipline of perseverance, embracing difficulty to build character, learning to forgive, developing a servant's heart, becoming more aware of God's presence, and developing our spiritual calling, mission, and purpose.[6] A crucial part of sacred marriage therefore is learning how to serve our spouses with a true servant's heart. Let's look at this topic more carefully.

Serving My Spouse

In sacred marriage, the key question is "How can I serve my mate?"[7] Thomas writes: "Marriage creates a situation in which our desire to be served and coddled can be replaced with a more noble desire to serve others—even to sacrifice for others. This is a call for both husbands and wives. . . . Kathleen and Thomas Hart refer to the 'paschal mystery' of marriage—the process of dying and rising as a pattern of life for married people. Each day we must die to our own desires and rise as a servant. Each day we are called to identify with the suffering Christ on the cross, and then be empowered by the resurrected Christ. We die to our expectations, our demands, and our fears. We rise to compromise, service, and courage."[8]

Thomas also emphasizes the need to not just engage in a servant's actions but also to have the right Christlike servant's attitude or spirit toward our spouses in sacred marriage, regardless of how our spouses may treat us at that particular moment when we are reaching out in loving service to them. He describes how as servants of Christ we can humbly give and serve our spouses in areas such as money, time, and sex. He concludes: "household chores, conversation, time, money—enter into these areas of need in your marriage with a desire to grow in the grace of giving. Pray that God might use them to root out your selfishness and to teach you to become gentle, forgiving, gracious, and kind."[9]

It is no wonder then that Paul Stevens tells the story of a visit he made with his wife, Gail, to the Wedding Church in Cana of Galilee when they were celebrating their twenty-fifth wedding anniversary and how the resident Roman Catholic clergyman Brother Joseph responded when told of their anniversary: "Mama mia," he said, "twenty-five years of martyrdom!" When he was introduced to Gail's parents who had just celebrated their fiftieth wedding anniversary, Brother Joseph responded: "Mama mia, a fifty-year martyrdom!" They ended up laughing with him uproariously, but knowing that he was right.[10] Marriage involves "martyrdom" on a daily basis: death and life, crucifixion and resurrection! Servanthood in marriage is therefore crucial for true success in marriage.

In *The Marriage Builder*, Larry Crabb pointed out that in order to achieve the fundamental goal in Christian marriage of ministering to your spouse's deepest needs (remembering that only the Lord alone can meet our deepest needs), the following three elements are essential or necessary: (1) a decision to minister to (or help or serve) your spouse; (2) an awareness of your partner's needs (which should be communicated and clarified); and (3) a conviction that you are God's chosen instrument to minister to your spouse.[11]

In order to minister to our spouses' deepest needs, in servanthood in marriage, we need to be aware of their love language or languages. Gary Chapman, in *The Five Love Languages*,[12] has described five major ways we can express our heartfelt commitment to our mates: (1) *words of affirmation*, or encouragement or appreciation that can be expressed verbally or in written form; (2) *quality time* in which you give your spouse undivided attention or focused attention; (3) *gifts or gift-giving*, which can come in many forms, including companionship and participating in activities for the sake of your mate; (4) *acts of service* in which you do concrete things that your spouse would like to have done such as mowing the lawn, cooking a meal, or taking out the trash; (5) *physical touch*, such as a hug or a squeeze of the hand. We may prefer different love languages from our spouses, so it is crucial for us as servants to minister to our spouses in *their* preferred love languages, and not ours. For example, if your spouse prefers the love language of acts of service more than words of affirmation, it may be more helpful to do concrete things for your spouse rather than just verbally express your love or appreciation. I am a verbally expressive person, and I have been told by my wife on some days that I have already said, "I love you" several times to her and that I don't need to "oversay" it! She would prefer then that I do some concrete acts of service instead, such as taking out the trash or washing the dishes! Servanthood in marriage includes being sensitive to your spouse's needs and love languages.

Les and Leslie Parrott have further pointed out that you also need to speak your spouse's spiritual language, not just his or her love language. They wrote: "One of the single biggest stumbling blocks to spiritual intimacy in a marriage is a failure to understand and appreciate the other's spiritual language. In other words, if we don't recognize that our partner's means of communion with God is valid, we discount it. Intentionally or not, we send a message to our partner that says *you don't know God like I do*."[13] They suggest that we be sensitive to at least nine spiritual pathways to God, based on the description of several distinct spiritual temperaments that Thomas provided in *Sacred Pathways*, a book that emphasizes that spirituality is not "one-size-fits-all."[14] The nine spiritual pathways are the pathways of tradition, vision, relationships, intellectual thought, service, contemplation, activism, nature, and worship. We therefore need to allow our spouses to develop their spirituality in Christ in their own unique ways and not impose our preferred spiritual language or pathway on them.

Benefits of Sacrifice

Servanthood in marriage, including sacrifice or sacrificial attitudes and actions in marriage, is not only taught and emphasized in Scripture, but it has also been studied and supported in marital research. Scott Stanley, a well-known Christian psychologist specializing in research on marital success and failure, has summarized the marital research findings generally supporting the benefits or blessings of sacrifice in marriage. For example, people who were the most comfortable with the idea of sacrificing for their spouses were the ones who tended to be the most committed to each other, the happiest together, and the most self-disclosing in their marriages. Furthermore, sacrificial attitudes and actions were more likely to be found in happy, committed people.[15]

It is encouraging to know that marital research generally supports the benefits of sacrifice or servanthood in marriage. However, such sacrificial giving in marriage also requires wisdom to keep proper limits or boundaries, for example, as Stanley pointed out, not to sacrificially give to a spouse abuser who can end up harming the spouse physically.[16] Staying in such potentially dangerous situations of spouse abuse can result in serious physical injury, and sometimes even in death. Therefore, it may be wise, in such extreme situations, to physically separate from the spouse abuser and stay somewhere else safe, while trying to get some much needed professional help.

Stories of Servanthood in Marriage

Independently of Scott Stanley, I had decided to write about the amazing story and servanthood example of Robertson McQuilkin and how he served his wife, Muriel, who suffered from Alzheimer's disease for twenty-five years. I was therefore pleasantly surprised to read about this couple's experience and example in Stanley's book, *The Heart of Commitment*, as a powerful story of sacrifice in marriage.[17] *Christianity Today* has published three articles on their story.[18]

Robertson McQuilkin was serving as president of Columbia Bible College and Seminary (now Columbia International University) in South Carolina in the early 1980s when he first began to notice Muriel's memory deteriorating in small ways. Eventually she was diagnosed with Alzheimer's disease. Several years later Robertson made the amazing decision to resign as president and to personally take care of Muriel, his beloved wife. He was advised by many well-meaning people to get on with his life and his significant work and ministry. But he chose instead to go on living life together with Muriel, remembering his marriage vows that included for better or for worse, in sickness and in health.

Robertson also wrote about how Muriel's Alzheimer's disease progressed more slowly than usual. He therefore had the long, painful experience of watching her slowly lose almost all of her abilities and mental faculties. Muriel finally died on September 20, 2003, after years of sacrificial servanthood on the part of her husband in caring for her. He did not consider what he did sacrifice. But what he did is an amazing example of servanthood in marriage.

In the recent interview with Robertson shortly after Muriel's death, he said, "I don't feel like I've given anything up. Our life is not the way we plot it or plan it. And so I guess all along I've just accepted whatever assignment the Lord gave me. This was his assignment."[19] When asked, "What's next for you?," Robertson replied, "I don't try to project anything. I'm still getting it together. I found a wonderful quote from Mark Twain today that was a big help: 'It is one of the mysteries of our nature that a man, all unprepared, can receive a thunder-stroke like that and live. There is but one reasonable explanation of it. The intellect is stunned by the shock, and but gropingly gathers the meaning of the words. The power to realize their full import is mercifully wanting. The mind has a dumb sense of vast loss—that is all. It will take the mind and memory months, and possibly years, to gather together the details, and thus learn and know the whole extent of the loss.'"[20]

Stanley, commenting on the McQuilkin story, wrote: "I do know committed love often calls us to give in small ways that, in reality, are huge. When Robertson was changing diapers for Muriel, bathing her, holding her hand, speaking words of love to her, or doing any number of small acts to let her know she was not alone and that he cared for her body and soul, he was . . . acting on the deepest kind of committed love. It's often not grand theater—it's love and commitment acted on the small stages of life. . . . However, the committed life is about making the right choices about small things more often over time. That's called maturing."[21]

Another example of servanthood in marriage is that of Ruth Bell Graham, wife of Billy Graham. Ruth married Billy Graham in August 1943. Stanley wrote the following about Ruth Bell Graham in another significant story of sacrifice and service or servanthood in marriage: "She has made all the daily sacrifices of raising five children, and she has shared her husband with the rest of the world. . . . As I read about the Grahams, I could see that they have had a strong love and a sense of oneness from start to finish. . . . Billy and Ruth Graham have both done incredible things with their lives. Both have sacrificed a great deal, but their love is stronger for it. . . . Sacrifice is to love what exercise is to muscles. Sacrificially giving to each other is the expression of love, and it makes love grow."[22]

Servanthood in marriage that includes such sacrificial giving to one's spouse also applies to what Lee Strobel and his wife, Leslie, have called a spiritual mismatch in marriage between a Christian and a non-Christian spouse. In their helpful book, *Surviving Spiritual Mismatch in Marriage*, Lee and Leslie vulnerably describe how Leslie's decision to become a Christian resulted in great conflict with Lee, her skeptical and unbelieving husband. Leslie experienced loneliness, fear, perseverance, and faith as Lee experienced anger, resentment, conviction, and renewal. Today they are both Christians, and Lee has become an articulate spokesperson, evangelist, pastor, and apologist for the Christian faith.

Lee emphasized that a crucial factor that helped them survive their spiritual mismatch in marriage leading eventually to his becoming a Christian was Leslie's servanthood in marriage to him: "I was afraid that I was losing my wife to a rival male—Jesus—and this generated feelings of anxiety and insecurity in me. I was relieved to find, however, that Leslie's devotion to Christ actually reinforced her love for me and made her want to strengthen our bonds. . . . She lived out an attitude of gentle servanthood that put my needs ahead of her own. This is contrary to everything in our culture that tells us to selfishly put ourselves first—but that's what marriage is about. And it's what Christianity is about—following the Savior who 'did not come to be served, but to serve.' Leslie's constant efforts to reassure me of her love and devotion were vital in calming the turbulence of our relationship."[23] Leslie's servanthood in a spiritually mismatched marriage also included faithful and fervent prayer for her husband.

Lee also underscored the need to ask the most convicting question of all in order to have a truly successful marriage: "*How would I like to be married to me*?"[24] This question should be asked and pondered on a regular basis so that some painful, but helpful, self-examination can take place deep in our hearts. Such a process will help us to more humbly depend on God and to grow in servanthood in marriage, whether spiritually matched or mismatched.

Servanthood in Parenting

Another significant area of servanthood in the home is servanthood in parenting (e.g., see Eph. 6:4; Col. 3:21). Many parents, including Christian parents, focus on how they can bring up good children. They try to "perfectly" parent their kids so that the kids will turn out to be "perfect," well-adjusted, happy, and successful in life. Unfortunately, some parents try too hard and end up "hyper-parenting" their children and hurting them with too much stress or pressure, as Alvin Rosenfeld and Nicole Wise have pointed out.[25] Family psychologists and therapists have therefore often reminded parents that "good enough" parenting is really good enough! Efforts at "perfect" parenting will not only fail, because no one is perfect, but can lead to even more family problems.

Servanthood in parenting will therefore include a huge dose of realism as well as deep humility, depending on God for grace, love, and wisdom to be good enough parents to our children. As servants of Christ who are also parents, we realize that our children are gifts from God, not for us to hyper-parent or over-control or own, but to love and care for and even to learn from! Henry Nouwen has suggested that we view our children instead as "our most important guests."[26] He believes that this view of our children as guests can be a helpful and liberating one for parents because so many parents struggle with deep guilt over their children, feeling responsible for everything that their sons and daughters end up doing.[27]

Much good material is available from a Christian perspective on family life[28] in general as well as on parenting[29] in particular. As parents who are servants of Christ, we need to avail ourselves of helpful literature and guidelines that are biblically-based and scientifically or clinically sound, for being good enough parents to our children and teenagers, as well as for developing healthy and wholesome family relationships. We realize that we will need to serve our kids with love, wisdom, and sacrifice, and oftentimes with pain and humility as well. A crucial perspective to servanthood in parenting is what Thomas has called "sacred parenting,"[30] focusing on how raising children actually shapes our own souls as parents. In other words, it's not just about parents influencing and shaping children: children influence and shape parents, too!

Sacred Parenting and Sacrifice

A key verse Thomas cites is 2 Corinthians 7:1: "Dear friends, let us purify ourselves from everything that contaminates body and spirit, perfecting holiness out of reverence for God." He comments:

> At first this verse may not sound like a parenting verse (and in context it's not) but it may be the most helpful verse on parenting in the entire New Testament. Paul first tells us to focus on purifying *ourselves*, not our children. Many of us are tempted to focus on purifying *our children* that we neglect our own spiritual growth. . . . We must see parenting as a process through which God purifies *us*—the parents—even as he shapes our children. . . . This extensive purifying involves "everything that contaminates body and spirit." This takes us far beyond the obvious "physical" sins of substance abuse, physical abuse, sexual immorality, coarse language, and so on, and into more hidden contaminations of jealousy, fear, bitterness, resentment, control, and possessiveness. . . . Paul defines this process as "perfecting holiness." . . . This process of spiritual growth isn't just pervasive ("from everything that contaminates"), it's also ongoing ("perfecting," present tense). . . . What motivates us to approach parenting this way? Paul couldn't be clearer: we do it "out of reverence for God." When we are motivated out of reverence for God, we lose 99.9 percent of the excuses that we make in family life . . . *our own spiritual quest must drive our parenting*.[31]

Such sacred parenting, or servanthood in parenting, will often involve sacrifice. Thomas emphasizes that raising children teaches us to sacrifice, and thus we become even better servants of Christ to our children and family members! Some areas that require parental sacrifice include time, sex, prayer, finances, sleep, peace and quiet, and personal hobbies.[32] Sometimes, we may be called as parents to make major sacrifices in raising our children. However, more often we will be asked to make daily sacrifices on a small but still significant scale in our sacred parenting, such as a father choosing to play a board game with his daughter rather than watching television, or a woman getting home in time for dinner instead of working late.[33]

Paul Stevens has likewise noted that while much of the literature on Christian education in the home is focused on raising godly children, the Bible actually emphasizes raising godly parents: "Children are God's gifts to immature people to help them grow up. They are also God's gifts to help parents go deep with God. . . . Parenting is not *for* anything. It is not a contract with God in which one gives countless hours in order to turn out good children that rise up and call us blessed. It is a covenant experience of belonging in which God meets us and forms us in the nitty-gritty of family life. The big question in the end is not how the kids turn out, but how the parents turn out!"[34]

In a similar vein, Dan Allender has emphasized that as parents we need to allow God to use our children to help us to grow up into spiritual maturity. As servants of Christ in sacred parenting, we need to treasure what God is teaching us through our children's quirks, failures, and normal childhood dilemmas, rather than fretting over whether we are doing everything right or perfect as parents. Allender especially challenges us to let go of the pressure of trying so hard to make sure that our children succeed, and instead learn to truly and deeply listen to each of our children. We need to listen to two core questions that he points out every child is asking: "Am I loved?" and "Can I get my own way?"[35] He concludes: "If we learn to listen to our children, we will find a precious truth: What they deeply crave is the same core desire we find in *our own hearts*. As we listen, we will learn to ask the same questions of the God who has made us and called us to be parents. We will ask him if he will still delight in us if we take great risks, discard some venerated rules, and sometimes fail miserably in our efforts to raise our children well. And we'll learn to listen to his answer to us: '*Yes*, you are loved more than you can ever fathom', and '*No*, you can't have your own way. But as you pursue my way, you will find the deepest satisfaction your heart can ever know.'"[36] Servanthood in parenting means engaging often in such deep and loving listening to our children.

Honoring Our Children

The importance of honor in our relationships with our children, and especially our teenagers, has been emphasized by Gary Smalley and his son Greg Smalley in a book on fostering a great relationship with your teen. They note that both their experience and research "indicate that increasing honor and decreasing anger in the home are the two main principles in raising healthy teenagers."[37] They see honor as a gift we give to others, and hence it is not dependent on their actions or on our feelings. They define honor as "deciding to place high value, worth, and importance on another person by viewing him or her as a priceless gift and granting him or her a position in our lives worthy of great respect. . . . At the heart of making others feel valuable, loved, and accepted is a decision to honor them, even above ourselves."[38] Servants of Christ will humbly and lovingly choose to honor others this way, including our children, spouses, and other family members, even our own parents.

Honoring Our Parents

Honoring our parents is actually even more crucial because it is one of the Ten Commandments that God has given us! In Exodus 20:12 we read, "Honor your father and your mother, so that you may live long in the land the Lord your God is giving you." Dennis Rainey has called this the "forgotten commandment." In *The Tribute*, he writes: "Instead of honoring our parents, we've taken the better part of the past three decades to bash, blame, and attack our parents for their faults and failures. . . . We have failed to obey that which God clearly commands: to honor our parents."[39] Rainey goes on to suggest that honoring our parents means to give them three gifts: understanding, compassion, and forgiveness.[40] Writing a tribute to our parents is one concrete way of honoring them.

Another important way in which we, as servants of Christ, can honor our parents is in caring for them in their latter years when they are aging or aged. It will involve sacrifice of various sorts. Whether we have them stay with us in our homes, or place them in a retirement home or even in a convalescent nursing home, we need to continue to love them and care for them. Terry Hargrave has written a recent book on such servanthood to aging parents, *Loving Your Parents When They Can No Longer Love You.*[41] In doing this, we continue to honor our parents as God has commanded us to.

I am aware that there may be some painful and broken family situations where parents have been terribly abusive or disturbed, and it may not be possible or safe to maintain contact with them. With the help of the Holy Spirit and the grace of God, we can still honor such parents by extending the gifts of understanding, compassion, and especially forgiveness to them.

Servanthood in the home includes servanthood in marriage, or sacred marriage; servanthood in parenthood, or sacred parenting; honoring our children, spouses, and other family members including siblings; and honoring our parents, aging or aged. Servanthood begins at home! But it should never end at home. Servanthood in the home is connected to servanthood in the church and community as well as to servanthood in the workplace and school, which is our topic for the next chapter.

13

Servanthood in the Workplace and School

Anointed for business. Marketplace spirituality and ministry. Serving God at work—because your work matters to God! God at work—the Monday connection. In fact, the other six days after Sunday! These are topics and some actual titles of books that have received increasing attention and treatment in recent years—and rightly so. There is a tendency in the church and Christian circles to view the marketplace where the business of life is conducted in the workplace and school as inferior or second-class "work," compared to so-called "full-time Christian ministry," especially as a pastor, church worker, or missionary. In fact, a very dangerous, potentially harmful, and usually erroneous distinction has been made between secular work in the marketplace and sacred work in the church or church-related ministries. It is therefore refreshing that in the last few years work in the marketplace, whatever the profession or position, whether brick-layer, banker, beautician, barber, baker, or businessperson, is now increasingly being viewed as equally sacred. Of course there are some professions that cannot be seen as sacred at all, such as prostitution and drug-dealing, witchcraft or psychic fortune-telling. However, the majority of legitimate forms of employment or work can be sacred under the lordship of Christ. As servants of Christ, we have therefore been called by him to be involved in servanthood in the workplace and school, or ministry in the marketplace. Before we delve more deeply into what servanthood in the workplace and school may mean, we need to first be clear about what being called by the Lord is all about.

Os Guinness, in *The Call*, has provided much helpful clarification and insight into what the core of our calling, or call, from God really means, referring to finding and fulfilling the central purpose of our lives. First, he defines calling this way: "Calling is the truth that God calls us to himself so decisively that everything we are, everything we do, and everything we have is invested with a special devotion, dynamism, and direction lived out as a response to his summons and service."[1] Guinness goes on to differentiate between primary and secondary calling: "Our primary calling as followers of Christ is by him, to him, and for him. First and foremost we are called to someone (God), not to something (such as motherhood, politics, or teaching), or to somewhere (such as the inner city or Outer Mongolia). . . . Our secondary calling, considering who God is as sovereign, is that everyone, everywhere, and in everything should think, speak, live, and act entirely for him. We can therefore properly say as a matter of secondary calling that we are called to homemaking or to the practice of law or to art history. But these and other things are always the secondary, never the primary calling. They are 'callings' rather than the 'calling'. They are our personal answer to God's address, our response to God's summons. Secondary callings matter, but only because the primary calling matters most."[2]

The challenge before us as Christians, and as servants of Christ, is to put first things first: We need to make our primary calling primary, focusing on worship and dedication to Jesus our best friend and first love! As Guinness puts it: "There is no surer guide here than the devotional writer Oswald Chambers. 'Beware of anything that competes with loyalty to Jesus Christ,' he wrote. 'The greatest competitor of devotion to Jesus is service for Him. . . . The one aim of the call of God is the satisfaction of God, not a call to do something for Him.' . . . Do we enjoy our work, love our work, virtually worship our work so that our devotion to Jesus is off-center? Do we put our emphasis on service, or usefulness, or being productive in working for God—at his expense? Do we strive to prove our own significance? To make a difference in the world? To carve our names in marble on the monuments of time? . . . The call of God blocks the path of all such deeply human tendencies. We are not primarily called to do something or go somewhere; we are called to Someone. We are not called first to special work but to God. The key to answering the call is to be devoted to no one and to nothing above God himself."[3]

To paraphrase or rephrase A. W. Tozer, we can be so preoccupied with the work of the Lord, that we forget the Lord of the work! Our first love and deepest devotion should always be dedicated to Jesus only, not to service or ministry or even servanthood. Out of our intimate, loving relationship with him, and that and only that is our primary calling, will come forth our secondary callings involving various ways of servanthood in the marketplace, whether at work or at school. We will now take a closer look at servanthood in the workplace.

Servanthood in the Workplace

Several books have recently been published emphasizing the sacredness of work and the importance of our work to God: our work matters to God and he has called us (secondary calling) and anointed us for business in the marketplace or workplace to be his servants in the world![4]

A Biblical Perspective on Work

Paul Stevens has provided a helpful biblical perspective on work, emphasizing several important points. First, God is the first worker as well as the best worker, and he calls us to work with him: "The Bible opens with God hard at work, crafting things and people (Gen. 2:7). . . . The Bible ends with God still at work recreating and transfiguring what he and his creatures have made—a city of exquisite beauty (Revelation 21–22). Apart from keeping the Sabbath, which turns out to be the meaning of both God's work and ours, God never stops working. Neither does Jesus (John 5:17); nor should humankind, because work is not only our duty but our dignity. It is a place to meet God. Indeed we actually do the work of God with God."[5] Second, work in and of itself, apart from God, is actually vanity: useless and meaningless as the writer of Ecclesiastes emphasizes (Eccles. 2:11, 22–23).[6] Third, work can only be meaningful and sacred, blessed by God, if we allow work as "an evangelist" to point us to Christ, so that we find in him what we cannot find in work. Stevens notes that it is work or labor done in "faith, hope, and love" (1 Thess. 1:3) that is ultimately meaningful and sacred, because it is "labor in the Lord" that is not a vain or empty thing (1 Cor. 15:58).[7] He therefore concludes: "Work is one context in which we meet, love, and serve God. God invites us to be subcreators, sharing God's work of developing the earth's potential and making God's world 'work'. Far from being a diversion from the spiritual life, work takes us directly to God through its creative possibilities and its purifying pressures. That is the soul of work. We work *with* God and *for* God."[8]

Stevens elsewhere refers to the rich metaphors in the Old Testament that describe God as worker, builder/architect, composer and performer, metalworker, garment maker and dresser, potter, farmer, shepherd, tentmaker and camper.[9] He emphasizes that the biblical answer to the question "What is the work of God?"

is much more inclusive than simply evangelism or "saving souls," and includes many other activities.[10]

Sacred Work

As servants of Christ we can therefore be involved in servanthood at work, in many different types of occupations or professions, working with God and for God. We will also realize that work can be viewed as sacred work that will help us to grow and mature in Christ through its trials, challenges, and pressures just as in sacred marriage and sacred parenting in servanthood in the home! Stevens writes in *Down-to-Earth Spirituality*: "Maturity is not something that can be obtained through self-help books, high-powered seminars and consumer-oriented religion. It comes only in the long, thick experiences of life, seasoned by some of the hardest and most disappointing experiences, which, if directed Godward, become the crucible for faith formation and true holiness. This can happen in our marriages (or singleness); it can also happen in the workplace."[11] And we can add, in the school or university for those of us who may be students or teachers or professors, serving the Lord in servanthood in the school or educational setting.[12]

In a similar vein, Doug Sherman and William Hendricks in an earlier book made the following conclusion about how God can use work to shape and mature us to become more like Jesus: "It should be clear by now that God uses everything in the workplace to train our character. He uses the evils we face, the people we can't stand, the circumstances of tension and pressure, the tedium of long afternoons, the solicitations to compromise, the irritations of angry customers, the interruptions, the financial reversals, the deals that fall through, even the traffic on the way home—He uses all of it to make us like Jesus."[13]

Stevens raises other crucial questions about work that will help us be better servants of Christ in the workplace and school:

What makes work God-blessed? And what makes work last or have eternal value? He provides the following biblically based answers: "What makes work God-blessed is not that God's Word and name are spoken out loud, but that the work is done with faith, hope, and love. With these virtues (which are not human achievements but divine encouragements), even slave work can become holy work. So Jacob's work life is an Old Testament hint of Paul's advice: 'Whatever you do, work at it with all your heart, as working for the Lord, not for men, since you know that you will receive an inheritance from the Lord as a reward' (Col. 3:23–24). . . . What makes work last is not the religious character of the work but the fact that it is done for Christ (1 Cor. 3:10–15). . . . The work may be sheep sorting or muffin making, selling or buying, processing information or food, creating a hospitable environment or building houses, teaching or doing accounts."[14] Ultimately then, all good work done for Christ is work that advances God's kingdom on earth.[15]

Mutual Respect and Wholehearted Service

Another key biblical text on work and servanthood in the workplace is Ephesians 6:5–9. In *The Message*, the text reads:

> Servants, respectfully obey your earthly masters but always with an eye to obeying the real master, Christ. Don't just do what you have to do to get by, but work heartily, as Christ's servants doing what God wants you to do. And work with a smile on your face, always keeping in mind that no matter who happens to be giving the orders, you're really serving God. Good work will get you good pay from the Master, regardless of whether you are slave or free. Masters, it's the same with you. No abuse, please, and no threats. You and your servants are both under the same Master in heaven. He makes no distinction between you and them.

Servanthood in the marketplace therefore means that both employees as well as employers or bosses need to treat each other with respect, and do their best in the power of the Holy Spirit, as serving the Lord Jesus himself—he is the real boss or Master!

Anointed for Business

Ed Silvoso has written an important book focusing on how Christians can use their influence in the marketplace to change the world, by the anointing and power of the Holy Spirit in the context of ongoing spiritual warfare in the boardroom. As servants of Christ in the workplace, we have been called and anointed for business! As Silvoso puts it: "To be anointed for business is to be set aside by God for service in the marketplace. Once anointed, we are to use our job as a ministry vehicle to transform the marketplace so that the gospel will be preached to, and heard by, every creature in our sphere of influence. The same principle applies to all areas of the marketplace: business, education and government. Anointing is an important subject in the Scriptures that is often associated with oil, which symbolizes the Holy Spirit."[16] Silvoso further notes: "As ministers of God, marketplace Christians need to know that spiritual warfare is a central component of their daily routines, whether they are aware of it or not. Satan and his evil forces constantly try to destroy lives and enterprises in the Church *but even more so in the marketplace*. . . . Since Satan is the source . . . the solution is the same: servants willing to turn the spiritual tide by ministering in the power of the Holy Spirit and setting free people who are oppressed by the devil."[17]

Types of Anointing in the Workplace

Silvoso also describes various types of anointing for doing business God's way and for letting our business or work be God's business and God's work, as we learn to serve him in the marketplace:[18] (1) *David's anointing*, or a kingly anointing that God gives to some of his servants to function in positions or roles of significant leadership in the marketplace or even in the nation; (2) *Esther's anointing*, in which you are empowered by God to protect your spouse with intercessory prayer, take good care of him or her, and wait for the right moment from the Lord to share wisdom, ultimately helping your spouse in his or her work in the marketplace; (3) *Priscilla and Aquila's anointing*, in which God calls and anoints a married couple to minister and work together in the marketplace, with an obvious need to nurture and protect the marital relationship in such a joint venture;[19] (4) *Lydia's anointing*, referring to being a businessperson, usually successful or wealthy but not necessarily, called and anointed by God to reach out to people who do not yet know Jesus personally, with hospitality and loving service; and (5) *The Little Servant's Anointing*, in which God calls and anoints humble, unknown people like the little servant girl in 2 Kings 5, and then places them in close proximity to people in powerful positions of leadership to eventually accomplish his will.

Silvoso concludes: "Whether you are a modern David, Esther, Priscilla, Aquila, Lydia, or little servant girl, recognize that God has anointed you for ministry in the marketplace and that such anointing must be used in the power of the Holy Spirit. Flowing in that anointing will protect you from deceit, inefficiency, and spiritual deadlock. . . . You are anointed for business—God's business. Your job is your pulpit, and the marketplace is your parish. You have been called by God to bring his Kingdom to the marketplace."[20] As servants of Christ in the workplace, we need to especially pray over every detail of our work or business, and pray for each one of our colleagues at work.

For those of us who may be called to positions of executive influence or leadership, perhaps with David's anointing, we need to be servants of Christ in how we engage in courageous leadership in the marketplace: as servants first who lead because God has called us and anointed us to lead, but always with a Christlike servant heart. Christopher Crane and Mark Hamel, in *Executive Influence*, focusing on how Christian executives can impact their workplace for Christ, pulled together the collective wisdom of more than fifty Christian executives or professionals in leadership positions in the marketplace, who are living out their faith as servants of Christ in various ways. Examples include sharing the gospel with people around them, encouraging spiritual renewal, maintaining high ethical standards in how they conduct their business, establishing corporate cultures that are faith-friendly, and investing personal and company resources in worthy causes that help make the world a better place.[21]

Business as Stewardship

Crane and Hamel emphasize that we need to approach business as stewardship, to handle our corporate responsibilities as a sacred stewardship entrusted to us by the Master himself, as his servants in this world.[22] We have therefore been called and anointed by God to serve as stewards in the workplace if that is where God has placed us, which is true for the majority of us who work for a living! Dennis Bakke, former CEO of the AES Corporation, has noted that ninety percent of the people in business believe that their purpose is to make money for their shareholders and themselves. He believes, however, that this should not be the main purpose of a corporation or individual involved in business: it should instead be to make the world a better place, based on a biblical understanding of stewardship.[23]

As servants of Christ who are also called to be stewards in the workplace, viewing business in the marketplace as a sacred stewardship, we need especially to be faithful (1 Cor. 4:2) over the long haul as we manage God's resources. In setting as our goal to make this world a better place rather than simply to make money (although making money is not wrong per se), as Bakke has advocated, we still need to know how to handle money and financial or material resources.

Joyful Giving

While it is crucial to be wise in how we continue to invest in the business world in order to responsibly grow our financial resources, it is also important for us to learn the deep joy of giving as we steward and use God's money and resources to help make this world a better place for his glory and the blessing of others. Servanthood in the workplace will include generously, joyfully, and sacrificially giving away our financial resources as God has blessed and prospered us, for his greater and eternal kingdom purposes. Randy Alcorn has written a powerfully helpful little book, *The Treasure Principle*, that focuses on discovering the secret of joyful giving from a biblical perspective. He defines the treasure principle thus: "You can't take it with you—but you *can* send it on ahead."[24] We need to realize that we cannot take any of our money with us when we leave this world at the end of our lives. But we sure can send it on ahead before the end of our lives by giving it away (at least 10 percent of every wage and gift received) for worthy causes and investing it for God's eternal purposes! Alcorn then presents the following six keys to the treasure principle: "(1) God owns everything. I'm His money manager. (2) My heart always goes where I put God's money. (3) Heaven, not earth, is my home. (4) I should live not for the dot (life on earth) but for the line (life in heaven). (5) Giving is the only antidote to materialism. (6) God prospers me not to raise my standard of living, but to raise my standard of giving."[25]

Our giving must extend especially to helping the poor and the oppressed in our society. Servanthood in the marketplace therefore includes what Ronald Sider has called "just generosity," stretching us to serve our society and the world at large. Public policy and justice issues are crucial ones for servants of Christ to deal with.[26] We are all challenged to do what the Lord requires of us: "To act justly and to love mercy and to walk humbly with your God" (Micah 6:8b). Servanthood in Christ therefore includes being involved in social concern and social action.

Servanthood in the School

Much of what has been covered on servanthood in the workplace also applies to servanthood in the school setting, including all levels of education, whether preschool, elementary school, junior high and high school, technical training or trade school, and university at both undergraduate and graduate levels. We may be students or teachers, administrators or support staff, in an educational or school setting. We can serve one another in many ways in such a context. For example, we can pray for one another; affirm and honor each other; help one another, including providing free tutoring where needed; listen to each other; smile as we go about doing our duties; take our studies seriously and do our homework; teach and do research well and mentor students; do administration and other routine tasks efficiently, effectively, and ethically; lead courageously but always with a servant heart or attitude; and be engaged in true service with deep love and humility by the power of the Holy Spirit, and not in self-righteous service.

Cornelius Plantinga, president of Calvin Theological Seminary in Grand Rapids, Michigan, has some wise words for us in the context of Christian higher education and lifelong learning which should characterize the humble, teachable posture of all true servants of Christ:

> Where learning is concerned, faithfulness means keeping at it long after a terminal degree. This means that even if you aren't thinking of pursuing graduate studies, your education ought never to end. Learning is a lifelong endeavor . . . learning isn't just for

> self-fulfillment or career enhancement. We learn in order to throw ourselves into the battle for the kingdom of God. . . . And it *is* a battle. The kingdom of God is in ceaseless conflict with the kingdoms of this world. The kingdoms of the world, the flesh and the devil oppose the kingdom of God with all the powers they can muster. Education for the sake of the kingdom isn't a wholly safe undertaking. A Christian who goes to work for the kingdom simultaneously goes to war. What's needed on God's side are well-educated warriors. . . . That's what Christian higher education is for. That's what all Christian education is for. Seen at its broadest reach, Christian education is for the kingdom of God.[27]

We have now covered servanthood in the church (chapter 11), in the home (chapter 12), and in the workplace and school in this chapter. In concluding this book on servanthood, the final chapter will deal with the very essence or core of servanthood and devoted discipleship in Christ: living for eternity.

14

Living for Eternity

Ultimately, servanthood is about living for eternity. As true servants of Jesus Christ, we have fallen deeply in love with him. We serve and obey him, our best friend, as citizens of heaven to come (Phil. 3:20–21) and pilgrims on earth in a journey of faith. We no longer live by the world's values, such as the idols of money, sex or pleasure, and power, but by eternal values, focusing especially on love or the currency of heaven, and the eternal destinies of human lives. We know that we need to be heavenly-minded enough in order to continue to be of earthly good. We realize the truth of what the apostle Paul emphasized: we need to be heavenly minded and think more often of heaven and the glory that shall be revealed in us, in order to better endure the sufferings of this present life, and therefore to continue to be of earthly good! In Romans 8:18, Paul wrote: "I consider that our present sufferings are not worth comparing with the glory that will be revealed in us." And in 2 Corinthians 4:16–18, Paul states: "Therefore we do not lose heart. Though outwardly we are wasting away, yet inwardly we are being renewed day by day. For our light and momentary troubles are achieving for us an eternal glory that far outweighs them all. So we fix our eyes not on what is seen, but on what is unseen. For what is seen is temporary, but what is unseen is eternal."

Living by Faith in Future Grace

John Piper has provided some deep insights from Scripture on the purifying or sanctifying power of living by faith in future grace that are crucial for servants of Christ to understand and appropriate as we live for eternity. He writes:

> I pray that you will hear and follow the call to find your joy in all that God promises to be for you in Jesus. And I pray that the expulsive power of this new affection will go on freeing you from the fleeting pleasures of sin and empower you for a life of sacrificial love. If, in this way, we prove that God is prized above all things, then living by faith in future grace will be to the praise of his glory. For God is most glorified in us when we are most satisfied in him. . . . Past grace is glorified by intense and joyful gratitude. Future grace is glorified by intense and joyful confidence. This faith is what frees us and empowers us for venturesome obedience in the cause of Christ.[1]

In order to live for eternity as servants of Christ, we need to have faith in future grace, to truly trust God's promises and find our deepest joy in all that God promises to be for us in Christ. Piper, however, reminds us that we are still engaged in spiritual warfare while serving Christ on earth against Satan, our enemy: "What this means for living by faith in future grace is not only that it is a lifelong battle, but that it is specifically a battle *against sin* (which is the only condemning instrument Satan has), and a battle *for faith* (which Satan wants most to destroy)."[2]

Piper especially emphasizes how suffering shapes an unshakable faith in future grace: "God so values our wholehearted faith in future grace that he will, graciously, take away everything else in the world that we might be tempted to rely on—even life itself. His aim is that we grow deeper and stronger in our confidence that he himself will be all we need."[3]

John Eldredge has similarly challenged us to wake up to the glory of a heart fully alive in Christ, realizing especially that we are living in the thick of spiritual warfare day by day on earth: "This is the heart of our Enemy. He is determined to hinder and harm and ruin God's image bearers. To steal and kill and destroy. So let me say this again: the story of your life is the story of the long and brutal assault on your heart by the one who knows what you could be and fears it. I hope you are beginning to see that more clearly now. Otherwise, much of the Bible will not make sense to you. Much of your *life* will not make sense to you."[4]

In the midst of such spiritual warfare and daily struggle, how can we continue to grow in faith in future grace and hence live for eternity?

Keeping the Faith or Kept in the Faith?

My close friend, colleague, and prayer partner for over fifteen years, Jeff Bjorck, also a professor of psychology at Fuller Theological Seminary, preached a powerful and helpful sermon at Glendale Presbyterian Church in Glendale, California, on November 18, 2001, based on Hebrews 11, the well-known biblical text listing so-called "heroes and heroines" of the faith. Bjorck provided a freshly different, and I believe more biblically correct perspective on this text when he preached on "Keeping the Faith or Kept in the Faith?" He noted that when he recently did an internet search for the phrase "hall of fame," about 800,000 entries popped up, with over 500 different halls of fame! Hero worship is pervasive today. And we tend to view Hebrews 11 as a Hall of Faith or a List of Heroes of the Faith. In fact, Bjorck in another internet search for the phrase "hall of faith," found 561 listings!

Bjorck said in his insightful sermon: "Let me propose to you however, that Hebrews 11 is not intended as a description of heroes at all. . . . I propose that we consider Hebrews 11 as a wonderful 'List of Losers' . . . virtually every person mentioned in this passage was also mentioned elsewhere in 'The Story of God' regarding a major *failure*; not just an episode of rebellion, or a little mistake, but a MAJOR Failure . . . their collective lives illustrated humanity's need for grace and mercy far more than they depicted godliness, holiness, or righteousness."

Bjorck concluded his sermon with these encouraging words:

> I would suggest the wonderful news of Hebrews 11 is this: If God could give faith and work amazing miracles through ordinary human beings like King David, Samson, and others, then He can and will work through you and me. If God gives the *gift* of faith to people who clearly and continually fall short of His Holiness, then the faith you and I need can truly be experienced as a gift. We can stop conceptualizing faith as some precious substance that we have to manufacture to fill God's bucket of expectations. And THIS is good news! And THIS is what makes grace truly amazing! . . . Thus, our Hebrews author encourages us to . . . remain aware of our connection to a God whose love will never let us go, a God who will *keep you* in His hand. He promised that He will never leave us or forsake us, and He invites us to hold him at His Word!

Ultimately then, faith in future grace, or living for eternity as servants of Christ, is a gift or grace from a faithful God who will keep us in such faith. We are kept in the faith by him and his grace rather than we keeping the faith. We don't try to hang in there as much as he hangs in there with us and for us always—because Jesus has already hung for us 2,000 years ago on that cruel cross of Cavalry. But he will faithfully and lovingly and sometimes even severely through suffering (but always with severe mercy), stretch and grow this faith, this trust, this confidence, this capacity to really take him at his Word and bank our whole lives on his promises for us in Christ: faith in future grace!

More recently, Piper wrote about how to fight for joy in God, emphasizing that joy in God is really a gift of God that only God can truly create. However, he also describes how to use God's Word and prayer in the fight for joy. The aim of his book is "to sustain love's ability to endure sacrificial losses of property and security and life, by the power of joy in the path of love. The aim is that Jesus Christ be made known in all the world as the all-powerful, all-wise, all-righteous, all-merciful, all-satisfying Treasure of the universe."[5] This is also the aim of true servants of Christ who live for eternity and the joy of God in Christ. Elsewhere, Piper writes: "Remember, you have one life. That's all. You were made for God. Don't waste it."[6]

Heaven

Servants of Christ live their lives to the fullest, by living for eternity and ultimately for heaven to come. As such servants, we therefore do not waste our lives. We live with deep, assured hope of heaven to come, by faith in future grace that includes the promise of heaven.

Randy Alcorn, in his recent book *Heaven*, emphasizes that what the Bible actually says about heaven is often not what we usually assume about heaven, such as the following characteristics:

> New Earth; Familiar, earthly; Resurrected (embodied); Home (all the comforts of home with all the innovations of an infinitely creative God); Retaining the good; finding the best ahead; Time and space; Dynamic; Both old and new; A God to worship and serve; a universe to rule; purposeful work to accomplish; friends to enjoy; An eternity of learning and discovering; Fascinating;

> Continuous fulfillment of desire; and Presence of the wonderful (everything we desire and nothing we don't). . . . *When we die, believers in Christ will not go to the Heaven where we'll live forever.* Instead, we'll go to an intermediate Heaven. In the intermediate Heaven, we'll be in Christ's presence, and we'll be joyful, but we'll be looking forward to our bodily resurrection and permanent relocation to the New Earth. . . . If we fail to grasp this truth, we will fail to understand the biblical doctrine of Heaven.[7]

He further notes that our longing for heaven is really a longing for God himself.[8]

As servants of Christ who live for eternity, who long for God and heaven to come, we need to daily ask ourselves the following questions in light of heaven (and hell) as wisely advocated by Alcorn:

> Do I daily reflect on my own mortality? Do I daily realize there are only two destinations—Heaven or Hell—and that I and every person I know will go to one or the other? . . . Do I daily realize that my life is being examined by God, the Audience of One, and that the only appraisal of my life that will ultimately matter is his? Do I daily reflect on the fact that my ultimate home will be the New Earth, where I will see God and serve him as a resurrected being in a resurrected human society, where I will overflow with joy and delight in drawing nearer to God by studying him and his creation, and where I will exercise, to God's glory, dominion over his creation?[9]

Such questions will help us as servants of Christ to be heaven-minded, to serve and live for what will last for eternity, and not for the superficial and shallow pleasures of a fleeting and fallen world. As Alcorn beautifully puts it:

> What *will* last for eternity is every service to the needy, every dollar given to feed the hungry, every cup of cold water given to the thirsty, every investment in missions, every prayer for the

> needy, every effort invested in evangelism, and every moment spent caring for precious children—including rocking them to sleep and changing their diapers. . . . Pastors and church leaders should train themselves and their people to be Heaven-minded. This means teaching and preaching about Heaven. . . . What will last forever? God's Word. People. Spending time in God's Word and investing in people will pay off in eternity and bring me joy and perspective now.[10]

We read in Revelation 21:1, 3–5: "Then I saw a new heaven and a new earth. . . . And I heard a loud voice from the throne saying, 'Now the dwelling of God is with men, and he will live with them. They will be his people, and God himself will be with them and be their God. He will wipe every tear from their eyes. There will be no more death or mourning or crying or pain, for the old order of things has passed away.' He who was seated on the throne said, 'I am making everything new!' Then he said, 'Write this down, for these words are trustworthy and true.'" Alcorn challenges us to live every day in the light of these words, and to remember that we were made to live for Jesus and for heaven.[11]

With such tremendous hope and anticipatory joy in heaven to come, ultimately in the new earth, servants of Christ can be deeply encouraged to keep on serving, even if unsung, unnoticed, and unappreciated by people. Rick Warren points out: "In heaven God is going to openly reward some of his most obscure and unknown servants—people we have never heard of on earth, who taught emotionally disturbed children, cleaned up after incontinent elderly, nursed AIDS patients, and served in thousands of other unnoticed ways. Knowing this, don't be discouraged when your service is unnoticed or taken for granted. Keep on serving God!"[12] Arthur Roberts therefore reminds us: "The hope of heaven is a beacon guiding us on our earthly journey."[13]

Servanthood as Long as We Can

As servants of Christ, we will continue to serve him in true servanthood as long as we can on earth, till the end of our lives or until we see him face to face. Warren Wiersbe, in his helpful book, *On Being a Servant of God*, challenges us with this conclusion: "It has always taken courage and compassion for God's people to minister in any age. The sovereignty of God and the love of God make an unbeatable combination for any servant of God against which the devil has no power. So start ministering today and keep ministering as long as you can. There is no discharge in this war. . . . If we've done the will of God, we've helped prepare the way for the next generation, just as others prepared the way for us. The work goes on."[14]

As servants of Christ, we can also serve him as long as we can, with the deep assurance that he will take care of us or undertake for us, honor us, and give us his best. In Isaiah 54:17, we read: "'No weapon forged against you will prevail, and you will refute every tongue that accuses you. This is the heritage of the servants of the LORD, and this is their vindication from me,' declares the LORD." The latter half of this verse is rendered thus in *The Message*: "'This is what God's servants can expect. I'll see to it that everything works out for the best.' God's Decree" (Isa. 54:17b). And in John 12:26, Jesus challenges and reassures us as his servants: "Whoever serves me must follow me, and where I am, my servant also will be. My Father will honor the one who serves me."

Servanthood in Heaven

We also keep on serving the Lord in true servanthood on earth, as long as we can, because we know that we are being prepared to serve him forever and reign forever with him in heaven to come in the new earth! In Revelation 22:3–5, we read: "No longer will there be any curse. The throne of God and of the Lamb will be in the city, and his servants will serve him. They will see his face, and his name will be on their foreheads. There will be no more night. They will not need the light of a lamp or the light of the sun, for the Lord God will give them light. And they will reign for ever and ever."

Anne Graham Lotz encourages us with the following words: "God's children will be given positions of leadership and responsibility in the new earth so that we might uniquely serve Christ for all eternity. The highest positions of authority in the universe will actually be positions as household servants. No matter where our service takes us or what our service is, it will ultimately be for the glory of Christ. . . . But when we get to Heaven, there will be . . . no hidden agendas, no ulterior motives, no secret ambitions, no selfish pride. Everyone—*every single person*—will live and serve for the praise and glory of God's only Son, Jesus Christ!"[15] Servanthood in heaven will be with perfect joy and worship of God! There will no longer be any suffering or pain or crying or mourning because there will be no more sin. It will be better than anything else we have most deeply enjoyed or savored on earth—infinitely better in the perfect joy of the Lord in heaven or the new earth to come! We all long for home, for heaven or the new earth, believing that the best is yet to come. We are therefore enabled by God's grace to live lightly on earth, not clinging so tightly to life and our possessions, accomplishments, and even human relationships in this present world, as Mark McMinn has noted.[16]

A Personal Story

I would like to share a personal story about my brother, Siang-Yong Tan, who is professor of medicine and adjunct professor of law, and director of the St. Francis International Center for Healthcare Ethics, at the University of Hawaii in Honolulu, Hawaii. A few years ago, in an article he cited a letter of recommendation for an applicant to medical school at the University of California, Davis, in which a professor of biochemistry described the student he was recommending as having a "servant's heart." The professor went on to say that, as a patient, he would want to be cared for by a doctor who had a "servant's heart."[17] My brother was writing from a secular perspective, but emphasizing the need for altruism and excellence in the ethical practice of medicine. He was, in fact, advocating a kind of servanthood or "servant's heart" in medical practice! He sent me a copy of his article some time ago when he first heard that I was planning to write a book on servanthood and wondered if we were in the "same business" of servanthood.

My brother's conclusions in his article are worth quoting because of parallel dangers that are also present today in the Christian context of ministry, especially in the church: "The medical profession is under siege. The public increasingly distrusts us because we are too condescending to listen, too mediocre to keep up, and too greedy to truly care about their welfare. Once upon a time, there was an empathic, scholarly, humanist named Doc, but as he grew popular and successful, he began to trade in his badge of service. His descent was gradual, barely perceptible, but nonetheless real. Finally, he found himself transformed into an arrogant, incompetent, materialistic three-headed god. This describes some of us, but many more of our colleagues are falling. Now is the time to again wear that badge with humility, and renew our pledge to society."[18] These are powerfully incisive words that the medical profession needs to hearken to, in order to maintain its high ethical and professional standards of practice—with servanthood or a "servant's heart."

The Call to Servanthood in Christ

Similarly, in Christian ministry today, especially in the local church but even in the marketplace and the home, as we have grown popular and successful we may also have gradually descended into arrogance, incompetence, and materialism and traded in our badge of service and servanthood. If so, we need to repent, and respond afresh to the call and challenge to servanthood in Christ. The call to servanthood is even more crucial for Christians: it is a call to servanthood in Christ now and for eternity! It is a sanctified servanthood, in loving and humble obedience to the Lord Jesus Christ our best friend, leading to compassionate and caring service to others in need. It is an "impossible" kind of selfless and Christ-centered servanthood made possible only by abiding or living in Christ and being empowered by the Holy Spirit. It is servanthood that follows Jesus all the way by living in Jesus all the way. It is servanthood that involves living for eternity, with faith in future grace that includes the promise and assured hope of heaven to come. It is servanthood made possible purely by God's grace and the presence and power of the Holy Spirit. Such servanthood is the secret of the most fulfilling and joyful life we can ever experience on earth and in heaven to come.

Servanthood is also crucial to becoming and being the deep people that are desperately needed in our superficial society today.[19] True servanthood deepens us, because we learn to live for eternity and in the depths of God himself.

Warren issues the call and challenge to true servanthood in Christ this way: "Imagine what could happen if just ten percent of all Christians in the world got serious about their role as real servants. Imagine all the good that could be done. Are you willing to be one of these people? It doesn't matter what your age is, God will use you if you will begin to act and think like a servant. Albert Schweitzer said, 'The only really happy people are those who have learned how to serve.'"[20]

As servants of Jesus Christ, we are to be yielded vessels in the hands of our Potter, the Lord himself, who will mold us and make us more and more like him. We are precious to him, and he takes great delight in us who also delight most in him! Sam

Sasser wrote: "Yielded vessels—vessels who trust the Potter and submit to His direction and care—are the Potter's delight. They contain the excellency of His power, the wonder of His grace. The Potter's touch is unique. He produces servanthood, not service. He goes to the deepest roots of the heart to make corrections. He is after durability. To be anointed and consecrated to servanthood is an honor. Only the constant touch of the Potter can make this possible."[21]

The longing and desire of a true servant's heart is to hear the Master Servant, the Lord Jesus Christ, say one day soon: "Well done, good and faithful *servant*!" (Matt. 25:21, 23). Let us as servants of Christ live for eternity by living in and for him, now and forevermore. Jesus Christ, through the church, is the hope of the world, and *servants* are the hope of the church. And through the church, and in the marketplace and home as well, servants in Christ, empowered by the Holy Spirit, following Christ, are also the hope of the world. As Jack Hayford points out, such servants will be Spirit-formed in both the *purity* (character or being) and the *power* (ministry or doing) of Jesus Christ (John 14:12): in true and full-orbed Christlikeness or "Christ's fullness."[22]

Clive Carver recently resigned as president of World Relief in order to pursue his desire to pastor a local church. His words are a fitting conclusion to this book: "To me, if you can get people to sacrifice, practice servanthood and invade society, then I believe you can change the world."[23] May each of us, as servants of Christ, daily pray: "O Lord, make me a servant today." May we thus be involved in full service, moving from self-serve Christianity to total servanthood.

NOTES

Chapter 1: Jesus' Call to Servanthood

1. Kortright Davis, *Serving with Power* (Mahwah, NJ: Paulist Press, 1999), 93.

2. Lawrence O. Richards, *New Encyclopedia of Bible Words* (Grand Rapids: Zondervan, 1991), 554–55.

3. Steve Hayner, "Playing to an Audience of One," *World Vision Today* (Summer 1998): 5–6.

4. David Cape and Tommy Tenney, *God's Secret to Greatness: The Power of the Towel* (Ventura, CA: Regal, 2000).

5. Bill Hybels and Rob Wilkins, *Descending into Greatness* (Grand Rapids: Zondervan, 1993).

6. Richard J. Foster, "Growing Edges," *RENOVARÉ Perspective* 1, no. 2 (1991): 1, a publication of RENOVARÉ (an organization committed to spiritual renewal) located at 8 Inverness Drive East, Suite 102, Englewood, CO 80112–5624.

7. Marva J. Dawn, *A Royal Waste of Time: The Splendor of Worshipping God and Being Church for the World* (Grand Rapids: Eerdmans, 1999).

8. Bruce Wilkinson, with David and Heather Kopp, *The Dream Giver* (Sisters, OR: Multnomah, 2003).

9. Rick E. Ferguson with Bryan McAnally, *The Servant Principle: Finding Fulfillment Through Obedience to Christ* (Nashville: Broadman and Holman, 1999).

10. John Piper, *Desiring God: Meditations of a Christian Hedonist, Expanded Edition* (Sisters: Multnomah, 1996), 9.

Chapter 2: Learning from the Master Servant—Jesus

1. Bruce H. Wilkinson, ed., *Closer Walk: 365 Daily Devotions That Nurture a Heart for God* (Grand Rapids: Zondervan, 1992), 49.

2. Ralph P. Martin, *A Hymn of Christ* (Downers Grove, IL: InterVarsity Press, 1997), 288.

3. Ibid., 289–91.

4. James Houston, *The Transforming Friendship: A Guide to Prayer* (Oxford: Lion, 1989). Also see Larry Crabb, *The PAPA Prayer: The Prayer You've Never Prayed* (Brentwood, TN: Integrity, 2006) and his emphasis on putting relational prayer before petitionary prayer.

5. See Siang-Yang Tan and Douglas Gregg, *Disciplines of the Holy Spirit* (Grand Rapids: Zondervan, 1997).

Chapter 3: Serving Our Best Friend

1. Edward C. Zaragoza, *No Longer Servants, but Friends: A Theology of Ordained Ministry* (Nashville: Abingdon, 1999).

2. Dallas Willard, "Spirituality: Going Beyond the Limits," *Christian Counseling Today,* 4, 1 (1996): 18.

3. Dallas Willard, *The Spirit of the Disciplines* (San Francisco: Harper & Row, 1988), 158.

4. Richard J. Foster, *Celebration of Discipline,* rev. ed. (San Francisco: HarperSanFrancisco, 1988).

5. Tan and Gregg, *Disciplines of the Holy Spirit.*

6. For example, see Maxie Dunnam, *The Workbook on Spiritual Disciplines* (Nashville: The Upper Room, 1984); Donald S. Whitney, *Spiritual Disciplines for the Christian Life* (Colorado Springs: NavPress, 1991); John Ortberg, *The Life You've Always Wanted,* expanded ed. (Grand Rapids: Zondervan, 2002); and Charles R. Swindoll, *So, You Want to Be Like Christ: Eight Essentials to Get You There* (Nashville: W Publishing, 2005).

7. Richard J. Foster, *Prayer: Finding the Heart's True Home* (San Francisco: HarperSan-Francisco, 1992), 1–2.

8. Emilie Griffin, *Wilderness Time: A Guide for Spiritual Retreat* (San Fransisco: Harper-SanFrancisco, 1997).

9. David Runcorn, *A Center of Quiet: Hearing God When Life Is Noisy* (Downers Grove: InterVarsity Press, 1990).

10. Gary W. Moon, *Falling for God: Saying Yes to His Extravagant Proposal* (Colorado Springs: Shaw Books, 2004), 4.

11. Ibid., 131.

12. David G. Benner, *Surrender to Love: Discovering the Heart of Christian Spirituality* (Downers Grove: InterVarsity Press, 2003).

13. Anne Graham Lotz, *Just Give Me Jesus* (Nashville: Word, 2000), vi.

14. Anne Graham Lotz, *My Heart's Cry* (Nashville: Word, 2002).

Chapter 4: Servanthood Versus Servitude

1. Kenneth C. Haugk, *Christian Caregiving: A Way of Life* (Minneapolis: Augsburg, 1984), 1.

2. Ibid., 73.

3. Ibid.

4. Siang-Yang Tan, *Rest: Experiencing God's Peace in a Restless World* (Vancouver, BC: Regent College Publishing, 2003), 152–53.

5. Zaragoza, *No Longer Servants, but Friends.*

6. Ibid., 34. Also see Susan Nelson Dunfee, *Beyond Servanthood: Christianity and the Liberation of Women* (Lanham, MD: University Press of America, 1989).

7. Zaragoza, 35. Also see Jacquelyn Grant, "The Sin of Servanthood and the Deliverance of Discipleship," in *A Troubling in My Soul: Womanist Perspectives on Evil and Suffering*, ed. Emilie M. Townes (Maryknoll, NY: Orbis Books, 1993), 199–218. Quote is from p. 215.

8. Zaragoza, 36. Also see Ada María Isasi-Díaz, "Un Poquito de Justicia—a Little Bit of Justice: A Mujerista Account of Justice," in *Hispanic/Latino Theology: Challenge and Promise*, Ada María Isasi-Díaz and Fernando F. Segoria, eds. (Minneapolis: Fortress Press, 1996), 325–39.

9. Zaragoza, 38–39.

Chapter 5: Servanthood Versus Servant Leadership

1. Robert K. Greenleaf, *Servant Leadership: A Journey into the Nature of Legitimate Power and Greatness* (New York: Paulist Press, 1977), 13–14.

2. Robert K. Greenleaf, *The Servant as Leader* (Indianapolis: The Robert K. Greenleaf Center, 1991), 7.

3. Zaragoza, 42–44.

4. Greenleaf, *Servant Leadership*, 28–29.

5. Zaragoza, 44.

6. Ibid., 46–49.

7. Ibid., 51.

8. Ibid., 60.

9. Ibid., 51–59. Also see Ray S. Anderson, *The Soul of Ministry: Forming Leaders for God's People* (Louisville: Westminster John Knox Press, 1997); Bennet J. Sims, *Servanthood: Leadership for the Third Millenium* (Boston: Cowley Publications, 1997); Celia Hahn, *Growing in Authority, Relinquishing Control: A New Approach to Faithful Leadership* (Washington, D.C.: The Alban Institute, 1994).

10. Calvin Miller, *The Empowered Leader: 10 Keys to Servant Leadership* (Nashville: Broadman & Holman, 1995), 17–18.

11. Max De Pree, *Leadership Jazz* (New York: Dell Publishing, 1989), 10–11.

12. Max De Pree, *Leadership Is an Art* (New York: Dell Publishing, 1989), 11. Also see Max De Pree, *Leading Without Power: Finding Hope in Serving Community* (San Francisco: Jossey-Bass, 1997, 2003).

13. Hayner, "Playing to an Audience of One," 6.

14. Rick Warren, *The Purpose-Driven Life* (Grand Rapids: Zondervan, 2002), 257–58.

15. Ibid., 258–64.

16. Ibid., 265–70.

17. Larry Spears, ed., *Reflections on Leadership: How Robert K. Greenleaf's Theory of Servant-Leadership Influenced Today's Top Management Thinkers* (New York: Wiley, 1995), 4.

18. Ibid., 4–7.

19. James A. Autry, *The Servant Leader* (New York: Prima, 2001), 3–21.

20. James C. Hunter, *The Servant* (New York: Prima, 1998).

21. James C. Hunter, *The World's Most Powerful Leadership Principle: How to Become a Servant Leader* (New York: Crown Business, 2004).

22. Ken Blanchard and Phil Hodges, *The Servant Leader: Transforming Your Heart, Head, Hands, & Habits* (Nashville: J. Countryman, 2003). Also see Ken Blanchard and Mark Miller, *The Secret: What Great Leaders Know—and Do* (San Francisco: Berret-Koehler, 2004).

23. Walter C. Wright, *Relational Leadership: A Biblical Model for Leadership Service* (Carlisle, U.K.: Paternoster, 2000), 2.

24. Ibid., 13–17.

25. Ibid., 12.

26. John Stott, *Basic Christian Leadership* (Downers Grove: InterVarsity Press, 2002), 11.

27. Ibid., 114.

28. Bill Hybels, *Courageous Leadership* (Grand Rapids: Zondervan, 2002), 12, 26–28.

29. J. Robert Clinton, *The Making of a Leader* (Colorado Springs: NavPress, 1988), 14.

30. Robert Banks and Bernice M. Ledbetter, *Reviewing Leadership: A Christian Evaluation of Current Approaches* (Grand Rapids: Baker, 2004), 110–11.

31. Hybels, *Courageous Leadership*, 27.

32. Ibid., 27–28.

33. Ibid., 181–97. Also see James C. Collins, *Good to Great: Why Some Companies Make the Leap . . . and Others Don't* (New York: HarperCollins, 2001); Stephen Covey, *The 8th Habit: From Effectiveness to Greatness* (New York: The Free Press, 2004); Jean Lipman-Blumen, *The Allure of Toxic Leadership* (New York: Oxford University Press, 2004); Gary L. McIntosh and Samuel D. Rima, Sr., *Overcoming the Dark Side of Leadership* (Grand Rapids: Baker, 1997); Reggie McNeal, *A Work of Heart: Understanding How God Shapes Spiritual Leaders* (San Francisco: Jossey-Bass, 2000), and Samuel D. Rima, *Leading from the Inside Out: The Art of Self-Leadership* (Grand Rapids: Baker, 2000).

34. For example, see Laurie Beth Jones, *Jesus, CEO* (New York: Hyperion, 1995); Larry Julian, *God Is My CEO* (Avon, MA: Adams Media, 2001); Charles C. Manz, *The Leadership Wisdom of Jesus: Practical Lessons for Today* (San Francisco: Berrett-Koehler, 1998); and Lorin Woolfe, *Leadership Secrets from the Bible* (New York: Barnes & Noble, 2002).

35. James M. Kouzes and Barry Z. Posner, *The Leadership Challenge*, 3rd ed., (San Francisco: Jossey-Bass, 2002), 22. Also see James M. Kouzes and Barry Z. Posner, eds., *Christian Reflections on the Leadership Challenge* (San Francisco: Jossey-Bass, 2004).

36. John C. Maxwell, *The 21 Irrefutable Laws of Leadership* (Nashville: Thomas Nelson, 1998).

37. John C. Maxwell, *The 21 Indispensable Qualities of a Leader* (Nashville: Thomas Nelson, 1999), v-vi.

38. Ibid., 136–38.

39. Hybels, *Courageous Leadership*, 141–56.

40. Daniel Goleman, Richard Boyatzis, and Annie McKee, *Primal Leadership: Realizing the Power of Emotional Intelligence* (Boston: Harvard Business School Press, 2002).

41. Jeffrey P. Greenman, "*The Shape of Christian Leadership*." Revised version of inaugural address on February 10, 2004, as the R. J. Bernardo Family Chair of Leadership at Tyndale Seminary, Toronto, Ontario, Canada, 4, 7, 8–9. He is now associate dean of biblical and theological studies and professor of Christian ethics at Wheaton College.

42. Eugene Peterson, "Follow the Leader," *Fuller Focus* (Fall 2001): 31.

43. Aubrey Malphurs, *Being Leaders: The Nature of Authentic Christian Leadership* (Grand Rapids: Baker, 2003), 10, 14–22. Also see Henry T. Blackaby and Richard Blackaby, *Spiritual Leadership: Moving People on to God's Agenda* (Nashville: Broadman & Holman, 2001); Eddie Gibbs, *Leadership Next: Changing Leaders in a Changing Culture* (Downers Grove: InterVarsity Press, 2005); Henry Klopp, *The Leadership Playbook* (Grand Rapids: Baker, 2004); Harold Myra and Marshall Shelley, *The Leadership Secrets of Billy Graham* (Grand Rapids: Zondervan, 2005); and J. O. Sanders, *Spiritual Leadership* (Chicago: Moody, 1967, 1980).

44. Warren G. Bennis and Robert H. Thomas, *Geeks and Geezers: How Era, Values, and Defining Moments Shape Leaders* (Boston: Harvard Business School Press, 2002).

Chapter 6: True Service Versus Self-Righteous Service

1. Richard J. Foster, *Celebration of Discipline*, 128–30.
2. Nancy Leigh DeMoss, *Surrender: The Heart God Controls* (Chicago: Moody, 2003), 75–77.
3. Ibid., 79.
4. Ibid., 71–72.
5. Ibid., 64–66.
6. Bill Bright, "Ten Keys to Anointed Leadership," *Fuller Focus* (Fall 2001): 4–6. Also see Bill Bright, *The Journey Home: Finishing with Joy* (Nashville: Thomas Nelson, 2003).
7. Bill Hybels, *The Volunteer Revolution: Unleashing the Power of Everybody* (Grand Rapids: Zondervan, 2004), 32.
8. Ibid., 31. Also see Greg Ogden, *Unfinished Business: Returning the Ministry to the People of God* (Grand Rapids: Zondervan, 2003).
9. Hybels, *The Volunteer Revolution*, 44–45.
10. Foster, *Celebration of Discipline*, 128–30.
11. Ibid., 132.
12. Ibid., 134–40.
13. Ajith Fernando, *Jesus Driven Ministry* (Wheaton: Crossway Books, 2002), 167.
14. Ibid., 228.
15. Ibid., 57–60. Also see David G. Benner, *Surrender to Love: Discovering the Heart of Christian Spirituality* (Downers Grove: InterVarsity Press, 2003); *The Gift of Being Yourself: The Sacred Call to Self-Discovery* (Downers Grove: InterVarsity Press, 2004); and *Desiring God's Will: Aligning Our Hearts with the Heart of God* (Downers Grove: InterVarsity Press, 2005).
16. Edmund Chan, *Growing Deep in God: Integrating Theology and Prayer* (Singapore: Covenant Evangelical Free Church, 2002).
17. Warren, *The Purpose-Driven Life*.
18. Warren, *The Purpose-Driven Church* (Grand Rapids: Zondervan, 1995).
19. Warren, *The Purpose-Driven Life*, 236.
20. Ibid., 227–78.
21. C. Peter Wagner, *Your Spiritual Gifts Can Help Your Church Grow* (Ventura, CA: Regal, 1994).
22. Warren, *The Purpose-Driven Life*, 246–47.

Chapter 7: Servanthood and Suffering

1. Warren, *The Purpose-Driven Life*, 194.
2. Ibid., 195–96.
3. See *Christianity Today* (April 4, 1994): 6.
4. Paul Billheimer, *Don't Waste Your Sorrows* (Fort Washington, PA: Christian Literature Crusade, 1977), 81, 130, 121.
5. Joni Eareckson Tada and Steven Estes, *When God Weeps: Why Our Sufferings Matter to the Almighty* (Grand Rapids: Zondervan, 1997), 232–40.
6. Larry Crabb, *Shattered Dreams: God's Unexpected Pathway to Joy* (Colorado Springs: Water Brook Press, 2001), 4–5.
7. Ibid., 155, 157, 159. Also see Carol Kent, *When I Lay My Isaac Down: Unshakable Faith in Unthinkable Circumstances* (Colorado Springs: NavPress, 2004).
8. A. W. Tozer, *That Incredible Christian* (Beaverlodge, Alberta: Horizon House, 1977), 122, 124.

9. Foster, *Celebration of Discipline*, 102–4.

10. Gerald G. May, *The Dark Night of the Soul: A Psychiatrist Explores the Connection Between Darkness and Spiritual Growth* (San Francisco: HarperSanFrancisco, 2004), 4–6.

11. Ibid., see 98–99.

12. Alan E. Nelson, *Embracing Brokenness: How God Refines Us Through Life's Disappointments* (Colorado Springs: NavPress, 2002), 18.

13. Ibid., 31.

14. Ibid., 35–37.

15. Ibid., 104.

16. Ibid., 105.

17. Ibid., 108–16.

18. Gary L. Thomas, *Authentic Faith: The Power of a Fire-Tested Life* (Grand Rapids: Zondervan, 2002), 14.

19. Ibid., 14–15.

20. Ibid., 12.

21. Ross Paterson, *The Antioch Factor: The Hidden Message of the Book of Acts* (Tonbridge, Kent, England: Sovereign World, 2000).

22. Ibid., 234–35.

23. Erwin Raphael McManus, *An Unstoppable Force: Daring to Become the Church God Had in Mind* (Loveland, CO: Group Publishing, 2001), 23, 33.

24. Marva J. Dawn, *Powers, Weakness, and the Tabernacling of God* (Grand Rapids: Eerdmans, 2001), 59.

25. Ibid., 41.

26. Roy Clements, *The Strength of Weakness: How God Uses Our Flaws to Achieve His Goals* (Grand Rapids: Baker, 1995), 213.

27. J. I. Packer, *Rediscovering Holiness* (Ann Arbor, MI: Vine Books, 1992), 238.

28. Fernando, *Jesus Driven Ministry*, 52–53.

29. Ibid., 110.

30. Thomas, *Authentic Faith*, 58.

31. Ibid., 7–17.

32. dc Talk, *Jesus Freaks, Vol. II: Stories of Revolutionaries Who Changed Their World: Fearing God, Not Man* (Minneapolis: Bethany House, 2002), 352–53. Also see dc Talk, *Jesus Freaks* (Minneapolis: Bethany House, 1999).

33. John Stott, *The Message of Acts* (Downers Grove: InterVarsity Press, 1990), 119.

34. See Siang-Yang Tan, "Suffering and Worship," *Theology, News, and Notes* (October 1999): 17.

Chapter 8: Servanthood and Humility

1. Packer, *Rediscovering Holiness*, 251.

2. Ibid., 254–66.

3. C. Peter Wagner, *Humility* (Ventura, CA: Regal, 2002), 7.

4. Ibid., 8, 13.

5. Ibid., 38.

6. Ibid., 22.

7. Andrew Murray, *Humility* (New Kensington, PA: Whitaker House, 1982), 51.

8. Randy Rowland, *The Sins We Love* (New York: Doubleday, 2000), 7.

9. Mark McMinn, *Why Sin Matters: The Surprising Relationship Between Our Sin and God's Grace* (Wheaton: Tyndale, 2004), 67.

10. David Powlison, "Biological Psychiatry," *The Journal of Biblical Counseling* 17, no. 3 (1999): 8.

11. C. S. Lewis, *Mere Christianity* (New York: Macmillan, 1952), 109.

12. Stuart Scott, "Pursue the Servant's Mindset," *The Journal of Biblical Counseling* 17, no. 3 (1999): 10.

13. Wagner, *Humility*, 59–60.

14. Scott, "Pursue the Servant's Mindset," 11.

15. Wagner, *Humility*, 63–72.

16. Ibid., 62.

17. Ken Blanchard and Phil Hodges, *The Servant Leader*, 26.

18. Stephanie Forbes, *Help Your Self: Today's Obsession with Satan's Oldest Lie* (Wheaton: Crossway Books, 1996), x.

19. Ibid., see 63–151.

20. Ibid., see 177–92.

21. Carolyn Custis James, *When Life and Beliefs Collide: How Knowing God Makes a Difference* (Grand Rapids: Zondervan, 2001). Also see Simon Chan, *Spiritual Theology: A Systematic Study of the Christian Life* (Downers Grove: InterVarsity Press, 1998) and Eugene H. Peterson, *Christ Plays in Ten Thousand Places: A Conversation in Spiritual Theology* (Grand Rapids, Eerdmans, 2005) and *Eat This Book: A Conversation in the Art of Spiritual Reading* (Grand Rapids: Eerdmans, 2006).

22. McMinn, *Why Sin Matters*, 77.

23. Leslie Vernick, *How to Find Selfless Joy in a Me-First World* (Colorado Springs: Water-Brook, 2003), 17.

24. Gary L. Thomas, *Seeking the Face of God* (Eugene, OR: Harvest House, 1994), 15–18.

25. Ibid., 124, 131, 143.

26. Scott, "Pursue the Servant's Mindset," 12.

27. Ibid., 13.

28. Ibid., 13–14.

29. Ibid., 14.

30. Wagner, *Humility*, 77–98.

31. Richard J. Foster, "Growing Together," *RENOVARÉ Perspective*, 11, Vol. 1 (January 2001): 2, published by RENOVARÉ.

32. Richard J. Foster, "Growing Edges," *RENOVARÉ Perspective*, 11, Vol. 2 (April 2001): 1.

33. Ibid., 2.

34. Rory Noland, *The Heart of the Artist* (Grand Rapids: Zondervan, 1999), 58–69.

35. Philip D. Kenneson, *Life on the Vine: Cultivating the Fruit of the Spirit in CHRISTIAN COMMUNITY* (Downers Grove: InterVarsity Press, 1999), 212–18.

36. Vernon Grounds, "Faith to Face Failure, or What's So Great About Success?" *Christianity Today* (December 9, 1977): 13.

37. Simon Chan, *Spiritual Theology*, 75–76.

38. Sonja Steptoe, "The Man with Purpose," *Time* (March 29, 2004): 54–56. Also see Timothy C. Morgan, "Purpose Driven in Rwanda: Rick Warren's Sweeping Plan to Defeat Poverty," *Christianity Today* (October 2005): 32–36, 90–91.

39. Leigh DeVore, "Voice from a Distant Shore," *Charisma & Christian Living* (May 2004): 52.

40. Wagner, *Humility*, 49–50. Also see John W. Yates, III, "Pottering and Prayer," *Christianity Today* (April 2, 2001): 60.

41. Russ Busby, *Billy Graham: God's Ambassador* (Del Mar, CA: Tehabi Books, 1999).

42. Ibid., 22.

43. Ibid.

44. Ibid., 258. Also see Myra and Shelly, *The Leadership Secrets of Billy Graham.*

45. Noland, *The Heart of the Artist,* 76.

46. Ibid., 74.

47. Brennan Manning, *The Signature of Jesus* (Portland: Multnomah, 1992), 122–23.

Chapter 9: Servanthood and Rest

1. Tan, *Rest*, 147.

2. Ibid., 21.

3. Ibid., see 27–33.

4. Ibid., see 37–184.

5. Tan and Gregg, *Disciplines of the Holy Spirit*, 175.

6. Richard J. Foster, *Freedom of Simplicity* (San Francisco: Harper & Row, 1981).

7. Marva J. Dawn, *Keeping the Sabbath Wholly: Ceasing, Resting, Embracing, Feasting* (Grand Rapids: Eerdmans, 1989).

8. Archibald D. Hart, *Adrenaline and Stress*, revised and expanded (Dallas: Word, 1995), 167, 172.

9. Also see Daniel F. Kripke, et al., "Mortality Associated with Sleep Duration and Insomnia," *Archives of General Psychiatry*, 59 (February 2002): 131–36.

10. Archibald D. Hart, *The Anxiety Cure* (Nashville: Word, 1999), 199.

11. M. Robert Mulholland, Jr., *Invitation to a Journey: A Road Map for Spiritual Formation* (Downers Grove: InterVarsity Press, 1993), 12.

12. For example, see Paul Meier, et al., *Filling the Holes in Our Souls: Caring Groups that Build Lasting Relationships* (Chicago: Moody Press, 1992), and James Bryan Smith with Lynda Graybeal, *A Spiritual Formation Workbook: Small-Group Resources for Nurturing Christian Growth*, revised and updated edition (San Francisco: HarperSanFrancisco, 1999).

13. For example, see Ernest Boyer, Jr., *A Way in the World: Family Life as Spiritual Discipline* (San Francisco: Harper & Row, 1984), and Tim Kimmel and Darcy Kimmel, *Little House on the Freeway: 301 Ways to Bring Rest to Your Hurried Home* (Sisters: Multnomah, 1994).

14. For example, see Larry Crabb, *Connecting* (Nashville: Word, 1997), and *The Safest Place on Earth* (Nashville: Word, 1999). Also see Randy Frazee, *The Connecting Church: Beyond Small Groups to Authentic Community* (Grand Rapids: Zondervan, 2001), and *Making Room for Life: Trading Chaotic Lifestyles for Connected Relationships* (Grand Rapids: Zondervan, 2003).

15. For example, see Keith R. Anderson and Randy D. Reese, *Spiritual Mentoring: A Guide for Seeking and Giving Direction* (Downers Grove: InterVarsity Press, 1999); David G. Benner, *Sacred Companions: The Gift of Spiritual Friendship and Direction* (Downers Grove: InterVarsity Press, 2002); James M. Houston, *The Mentored Life: From Individualism to Personhood* (Colorado Springs: NavPress, 2002); and Paul D. Stanley and J. Robert Clinton, *Connecting: The Mentoring Relationships You Need to Succeed in Life* (Colorado Springs: NavPress, 1992).

16. Larry Crabb, *SoulTalk* (Nashville: Integrity, 2003).

17. Ajith Fernando, *Jesus Driven Ministry*, 164.

18. For example, see Hart, *Adrenaline and Stress* and *The Anxiety Cure*; also see Dwight L. Carlson, *Energize Your Life: Overcoming Fatigue and Stress* (Ross-shire, Great Britain: Chris-

tian Focus Publications, 2003); Mark McMinn, *Making the Best of Stress: How Life's Hassles Can Form the Fruit of the Spirit* (Downers Grove: InterVarsity Press, 1996); and Richard A. Swenson, *The Overload Syndrome: Learning to Live Within Your Limits* (Colorado Springs: NavPress, 1998).

19. Hart, *The Anxiety Cure*, 149–52.

20. See Siang-Yang Tan and John Ortberg, *Coping with Depression*, revised and expanded edition (Grand Rapids: Baker, 2004).

21. Noland, *The Heart of the Artist*, 73.

22. See Henry Cloud and John Townsend, *Boundaries: When to Say Yes, When to Say No to Take Control of Your Life* (Grand Rapids: Zondervan, 1992); *Boundaries with Kids* (Grand Rapids: Zondervan, 1998); *Boundaries in Marriage* (Grand Rapids: Zondervan, 1999); *Boundaries in Dating* (Grand Rapids: Zondervan, 2000); and *Boundaries Face to Face: How to Have That Difficult Conversation You've Been Avoiding* (Grand Rapids: Zondervan, 2003).

23. Walt Larimore with Traci Mullins, *10 Essentials of Highly Healthy People* (Grand Rapids: Zondervan, 2003).

Chapter 10: Servant Evangelism and Warfare

1. Kenneson, *Life on the Vine*, 136–37.

2. Steve Sjogren, *Servant Warfare: How Kindness Conquers Spiritual Darkness* (Ann Arbor: Servant, 1996), 83.

3. Ibid., 82–83.

4. Kenneson, *Life on the Vine*, 150–51.

5. Ibid., 145–51.

6. See Crabb, *Connecting*, *The Safest Place on Earth*, and *SoulTalk*.

7. Steve Sjogren, *Conspiracy of Kindness* (Ann Arbor: Servant, 1993), 22. Also see Steve Sjogren, *101 Ways to Reach Your Community* (Colorado Springs: NavPress, 2001), and Steve Sjogren, Dave Ping, and Doug Pollock, *Irresistible Evangelism: Natural Ways to Open Others to Jesus* (Loveland, CO: Group, 2004).

8. Sjogren, *Servant Warfare*, 14.

9. Ibid., 15.

10. For example, see the following books related to spiritual warfare: C. Peter Wagner, *What the Bible Says About Spiritual Warfare* (Ventura, CA: Regal, 2001); Tom White, *The Believer's Guide to Spiritual Warfare* (Ann Arbor: Servant, 1990), and *Breaking Strongholds* (Ann Arbor: Servant, 1993). Also see Chip Ingram, *The Invisible War: What Every Believer Needs to Know about Satan, Demons, and Spiritual Warfare* (Grand Rapids: Baker, 2006) and David Powlison, *Power Encounters: Reclaiming Spiritual Warfare* (Grand Rapids: Baker, 1995).

11. For example, see the following books on the power and ministry of the Holy Spirit: Jack Deere, *Surprised by the Power of the Spirit* (Grand Rapids: Zondervan, 1993) and *Surprised by the Voice of God* (Grand Rapids: Zondervan, 1996); Craig S. Keener, *Gift and Giver: The Holy Spirit for Today* (Grand Rapids: Baker, 2001); J. I. Packer, *Keep in Step with the Spirit* (Grand Rapids: Revell, 1984); and John White, *When the Spirit Comes with Power* (Downers Grove: InterVarsity Press, 1988).

12. David Shibley, *Once in a Lifetime: Seizing Today's Opportunities for the World Harvest* (Tonbridge, Kent, England: Sovereign World, 1997), 99–100.

13. See Tan and Gregg, *Disciplines of the Holy Spirit*, 217–18.

14. Philip Yancey, *What's So Amazing About Grace?* (Grand Rapids: Zondervan, 1997), 272.

15. Ibid., 70.

16. Ibid., 272, 274. Also see Philip Yancey, *Rumors of Another World: What on Earth Are We Missing?* (Grand Rapids: Zondervan, 2003).

17. Brian McLaren, "A Radical Rethinking of Our Evangelistic Strategy," *Theology, News, and Notes* (Fall 2004): 4–6, 22. Also see Brian D. McLaren, *More Ready Than You Realize: Evangelism as Dance in the Postmodern Matrix* (Grand Rapids: Zondervan, 2002) and *A Generous Orthodoxy* (Grand Rapids: Zondervan, 2004); Dan Kimball, *The Emerging Church: Vintage Christianity for New Generations* (Grand Rapids: Zondervan, 2003); Leonard Sweet, ed., *The Church in Emerging Culture: Five Perspectives* (Grand Rapids: Zondervan, 2003); and Elmer Towns and Ed Stetzer, *Perimeters of Light: Biblical Boundaries for the Emerging Church* (Chicago: Moody, 2004).

18. Eddie Gibbs, "Reinventing Evangelism," *Theology, News, and Notes* (Fall 2004): 19. Also see Eddie Gibbs, *Church Next: Quantum Changes in How We Do Ministry* (Downers Grove: InterVarsity Press, 2000).

19. Gibbs, "Reinventing Evangelism," 19–22.

20. Richard Peace, "Evangelism and Spiritual Formation," *Theology, News, and Notes* (Fall 2004): 12.

21. Ed Silvoso, *That None Should Perish* (Ventura: Regal, 1994), 57. Also see Ed Silvoso, *Prayer Evangelism* (Ventura: Regal, 2000).

22. For example, see Paul Little, *How to Give Away Your Faith*, expanded and updated edition (Downers Grove: InterVarsity Press, 1988), and Rebecca Manley Pippert, *Out of the Saltshaker and Into the World: Evangelism as a Way of Life* (Downers Grove: InterVarsity Press, 1999). Also see Bill Hybels and Mark Mittelberg, *Becoming a Contagious Christian* (Grand Rapids: Zondervan, 1994), and Mark Mittelberg, *Building a Contagious Church: Revolutionizing the Way We View and Do Evangelism* (Grand Rapids: Zondervan, 2000).

23. See Brad Kallenberg, *Live to Tell: Evangelism for a Postmodern Age* (Grand Rapids: Brazos Press, 2002), 127.

24. Hybels and Mittelberg, *Becoming a Contagious Christian*, 119–32.

25. Ibid., 39–50. Also see Mittelberg, *Building a Contagious Church.*

26. McLaren, *More Ready Than You Realize.*

27. Steve Sjogren, ed., *Seeing Beyond Church Walls* (Loveland, CO: Group, 2002), 27. Also see Bill Easum and Dave Travis, *Beyond the Box: Innovative Churches that Work* (Loveland, CO: Group, 2004), and Rick Rusaw and Eric Swanson, *The Externally Focused Church* (Loveland: Group, 2005).

28. Rick Warren, *The Purpose-Driven Church*, and Bill Hybels and Lynne Hybels, *Rediscovering Church* (Grand Rapids: Zondervan, 1995).

29. George Barna, *Grow Your Church from the Outside In* (Ventura: Regal, 2002).

30. Richard J. Mouw, *The Smell of Sawdust: What Evangelicals Can Learn from Their Fundamentalist Heritage* (Grand Rapids: Zondervan, 2000), 152. Also see Richard J. Mouw, *Calvinism in the Las Vegas Airport: Making Connections in Today's World* (Grand Rapids: Zondervan, 2005).

31. Hybels and Mittelberg, *Becoming a Contagious Christian*, 11–24.

32. Ibid., 24.

33. Busby, *Billy Graham: God's Ambassador*, 129.

34. Wilkinson, *The Dream Giver*. For his latest Dream for Africa projects visit www.dreamforafrica.com. Also see Bruce Wilkinson, with Brian Smith, *Beyond Jabez* (Sisters, OR: Multnomah, 2005).

35. Glen Stassen and David Gushee, *Kingdom Ethics: Following Jesus in Contemporary Context* (Downers Grove: InterVarsity Press, 2003).

Chapter 11: Servanthood in the Church

1. John Stott, "Foreword," in Steve and Lois Rabey, eds., *Side by Side, A Handbook: Disciple-Making for a New Century* (Colorado Springs: Cook and NavPress, 2000), 7–8.

2. George Barna, *The Second Coming of the Church* (Nashville: Word, 1998), x-xi.

3. Tim Stafford, "The Third Coming of George Barna," *Christianity Today* (August 5, 2002): 32–38.

4. Ibid., 38.

5. Ibid.

6. Ronald J. Sider, *Living Like Jesus: Eleven Essentials for Growing a Genuine Faith* (Grand Rapids: Baker, 1996), 167, 170, 173, 179–80.

7. George Barna, *Think Like Jesus* (Nashville: Integrity, 2003), 22–23.

8. Ibid. Also see George Barna, *Transforming Children into Spiritual Champions* (Ventura: Regal, 2003).

9. Fernando, *Jesus Driven Ministry*, 89–106.

10. Dallas Willard, *Renovation of the Heart: Putting on the Character of Christ* (Colorado Springs: NavPress, 2002), 235.

11. Ibid.

12. Ibid., 77–92.

13. Ibid., 240.

14. Ibid., 251. Also see Dallas Willard, *The Divine Conspiracy: Rediscovering Our Hidden Life in God* (San Francisco: HarperSanFrancisco, 1998), and *The Spirit of the Disciplines*.

15. Warren, *The Purpose Driven Church*, 102–106. Quote is from p. 106.

16. Ibid., 107.

17. Ibid., 48.

18. Ogden, *Unfinished Business: Returning the Ministry to the People of God*. Also see Hybels, *The Volunteer Revolution*.

19. Stephen A. Macchia, *Becoming a Healthy Church: 10 Characteristics* (Grand Rapids: Baker, 1998), 7.

20. Peter Scazzero with Warren Bird, *The Emotionally Healthy Church: A Strategy for Discipleship that Actually Changes Lives* (Grand Rapids: Zondervan, 2003), 20–36.

21. Ibid., 6.

22. Wes Roberts and Glenn Marshall, *Reclaiming God's Original Intent for the Church* (Colorado Springs: NavPress, 2004), 5.

23. See Oliver McMahan, *The Caring Church* (Cleveland, TN: Pathway Press, 2002). Also see Gary R. Collins, *How to Be a People Helper*, revised edition (Wheaton: Tyndale, 1995) and Siang-Yang Tan, *Lay Counseling: Equipping Christians for a Helping Ministry* (Grand Rapids: Zondervan, 1991).

24. Sider, *Living Like Jesus*, 179.

25. Ibid., 180.

26. Ibid., 17, 31, 41, 57, 73, 87, 102, 119, 138, 167.

27. David Fisher, *The 21st Century Pastor: A Vision Based on the Ministry of Paul* (Grand Rapids: Zondervan, 1996), 209.

28. For example, see Leith Anderson, *A Church for the 21st Century* (Minneapolis: Bethany House Publishers, 1992), and *Leadership That Works: Hope and Direction for Church and*

Parachurch Leaders in Today's Complex World (Minneapolis: Bethany House Publishers, 1999); Marva Dawn and Eugene Peterson, *The Unnecessary Pastor: Rediscovering the Call* (Grand Rapids: Eerdmans, 2000); John W. Frye, *Jesus the Pastor: Leading Others in the Character and Power of Christ* (Grand Rapids: Zondervan, 2000); Gene A. Getz, *The Measure of a Church: Following the One True Standard* (Ventura: Regal, 2001); E. Glenn Wagner with Steve Halliday, *Escape from Church, Inc.: The Return of the Pastor-Shepherd* (Grand Rapids: Zondervan, 1999), and *The Church You've Always Wanted: Where Safe Pasture Begins* (Grand Rapids: Zondervan, 2002).

29. See Getz, *The Measure of a Church*, 194–210.

30. Dawn and Peterson, *The Unnecessary Pastor*.

31. Chan, *Spiritual Theology*, 225.

32. See Dawn and Peterson, *The Unnecessary Pastor*, 4.

33. Anderson, *Leadership That Works*, 39–51.

34. Roberts and Marshall, *Reclaiming God's Original Intent for the Church*, 162. Also see David Hansen, *Loving the Church You Lead: Pastoring with Acceptance and Grace* (Grand Rapids: Baker, 2005).

35. Anderson, *A Church for the 21st Century*, 222–23, 232.

36. For example, see Eddie Gibbs, *Church Next*. Also see Reggie McNeal, *Revolution in Leadership: Training Apostles for Tomorrow's Church* (Nashville: Abingdon, 1998) and *The Present Future: Six Tough Questions for the Church* (San Francisco: Jossey-Bass, 2003).

37. Andy Crouch, "The Emergent Mystique," *Christianity Today* (November 2004): 36–41. Also see note 17 of Chapter 10.

38. See C. Peter Wagner, *Changing Church: How God Is Leading His Church into the Future* (Ventura: Regal, 2004) and *Churchquake!: How the New Apostolic Reformation Is Shaking Up the Church As We Know It* (Ventura: Regal, 1999).

39. Amy Sheng, "My Observation of Short-term Missions," *First Evangelical Church Association Bulletin*, Issue 20 (June 2004): 10.

Chapter 12: Servanthood in the Home

1. For example, see Tim Clinton and Julie Clinton, *The Marriage You've Always Wanted* (Nashville, TN: Word, 2000); Archibald D. Hart and Sharon Hart Morris, *Safe Haven Marriage: A Marriage You Can Come Home To* (Nashville: W Publishing, 2003); Les Parrott and Leslie Parrott, *Saving Your Marriage Before It Starts: Seven Questions to Ask Before (and After) You Marry* (Grand Rapids: Zondervan, 1995) and *When Bad Things Happen to Good Marriages: How to Stay Together When Life Pulls You Apart* (Grand Rapids: Zondervan, 2001); Gary Smalley, *Making Love Last Forever* (Dallas: Word, 1996) and *The DNA of Relationships* (Wheaton: Tyndale, 2004); Greg Smalley, *The Marriage You've Always Dreamed Of* (Wheaton: Tyndale, 2005); David Stoop and Jan Stoop, eds., *The Complete Marriage Book: Collected Wisdom from Leading Marriage Experts* (Grand Rapids: Baker, 2002); Neil Clark Warren, *The Triumphant Marriage: 100 Extremely Successful Couples Reveal Their Secrets* (Colorado Springs: Focus on the Family, 1995); and H. Norman Wright, *The Marriage Checkup* (Ventura: Regal, 2002).

2. For example, see Dan B. Allender and Tremper Longman III, *Intimate Allies* (Wheaton: Tyndale, 1995) and *The Intimate Mystery: Creating Strength and Beauty in Your Marriage* (Downers Grove: InterVarsity Press, 2005); Larry Crabb, *The Marriage Builder* (Grand Rapids: Zondervan, 1982); Scott Stanley, *The Heart of Commitment* (Nashville: Nelson, 1998); Paul Stevens, *Married for Good* (Downers Grove: InterVarsity Press, 1986), and *Marriage Spirituality: Ten Disciplines for Couples Who Love God* (Downers Grove: InterVarsity Press,

1989); and Gary Thomas, *Sacred Marriage: What If God Designed Marriage to Make Us Holy More Than to Make Us Happy?* (Grand Rapids: Zondervan, 2000).

3. Stevens, *Marriage Spirituality*, 149, 150.

4. Allender and Longman, *Intimate Allies*, 177–78.

5. Gary Thomas, *Sacred Marriage*, 22, 266, 267. In becoming a holy couple, spiritual direction or spiritual accompaniment in marriage can be a crucial part of the process. See David Benner, *Sacred Companions*, 185–204.

6. Thomas, *Sacred Marriage*, 9.

7. Ibid., 180.

8. Ibid., 186–87.

9. Ibid., 196.

10. Stevens, *Marriage Spirituality*, 155.

11. Crabb, *The Marriage Builder*.

12. Gary Chapman, *The Five Love Languages: How to Express Heartfelt Commitment to Your Mate* (Chicago: Northfield Publishing, 1992).

13. Les Parrott and Leslie Parrott, *When Bad Things Happen to Good Marriages*, 157–58. Also see Les Parrott and Leslie Parrott, *Love Talk: Speak Each Other's Language Like You Never Had Before* (Grand Rapids: Zondervan, 2004).

14. Gary Thomas, *Sacred Pathways: Discover Your Soul's Path to God* (Grand Rapids: Zondervan, 2000).

15. Stanley, *The Heart of Commitment*, 191.

16. Ibid., 190.

17. Ibid., 193–98.

18. See Robertson McQuilkin, "Living by Vows," *Christianity Today* (Oct. 8, 1990) and "Muriel's Blessing," *Christianity Today* (Feb. 5, 1996), and Stan Guthrie, "The Gradual Grief of Alzheimer's," *Christianity Today* (Feb. 2004): 64–65.

19. Guthrie, "The Gradual Grief of Alzheimer's," 64.

20. Ibid., 65.

21. Stanley, *The Heart of Commitment*, 197–98.

22. Ibid., 201–2.

23. Lee Strobel and Leslie Strobel, *Surviving a Spiritual Mismatch in Marriage* (Grand Rapids: Zondervan, 2002), 68.

24. Ibid., 117. Also see Les Parrott and Leslie Parrott, *Becoming Soul Mates* (Grand Rapids: Zondervan, 1995), 226.

25. Alvin Rosenfeld and Nicole Wise, *Hyper-Parenting: Are You Hurting Your Child By Trying Too Hard?* (New York: St. Martin's Press, 2000).

26. Henri Nouwen, *Reaching Out: Three Movements of the Spiritual Life* (Garden City, NY: Doubleday, 1975), 56.

27. Ibid., 57.

28. For example, see Jack O. Balswick and Judith K. Balswick, *The Family: A Christian Perspective on the Contemporary Home*, 2nd ed. (Grand Rapids: Baker, 1999); Judith and Jack Balswick, *Families in Pain: Working Through the Hurts* (Grand Rapids: Revell, 1997); and Gary R. Collins, *Family Shock: Keeping Families Strong in the Midst of Earthshaking Change* (Wheaton: Tyndale, 1995).

29. For example, see Dan B. Allender, *How Children Raise Parents: The Art of Listening to Your Family* (Colorado Springs: Water Brook, 2003); Judy and Jack Balswick and Boni and Don Piper, *Relationship-Empowerment Parenting: Building Formative and Fulfilling Relationships with Your Children* (Grand Rapids: Baker, 2003); R. Paul Stevens and Robert Banks, eds.,

Thoughtful Parenting: A Manual of Wisdom for Home and Family (Downers Grove: InterVarsity Press, 2001); David Stoop and Jan Stoop, eds., *The Complete Parenting Book: Practical Help from Leading Experts* (Grand Rapids: Baker, 2005); Gary Thomas, *Sacred Parenting: How Raising Children Shapes Our Souls* (Grand Rapids: Zondervan, 2004).

30. Gary Thomas, *Sacred Parenting*. Also see Dan Allender, *How Children Raise Parents*.

31. Thomas, *Sacred Parenting*, 19–21.

32. Ibid., 192.

33. Ibid., 188.

34. R. Paul Stevens, *Seven Days of Faith: Every Day Alive with God* (Colorado Springs: NavPress, 2001), 65, 73.

35. Dan Allender, *How Children Raise Parents*, 21.

36. Ibid., 27.

37. Gary Smalley and Greg Smalley, *Bound by Honor: Fostering a Great Relationship with Your Teen* (Wheaton: Tyndale, 1998), 4.

38. Ibid., 14.

39. Dennis Rainey, *The Tribute: What Every Parent Longs to Hear* (Nashville: Thomas Nelson, 1994), 3–4.

40. Ibid., 109.

41. Terry D. Hargrave, *Loving Your Parents When They Can No Longer Love You* (Grand Rapids: Zondervan, 2005).

Chapter 13: Servanthood in the Workplace and School

1. Os Guinness, *The Call: Finding and Fulfilling the Central Purpose of Your Life* (Nashville: W Publishing, 1998), 29.

2. Ibid., 31.

3. Ibid., 42–43.

4. For example, see Christopher A. Crane and Mike Hamel, *Executive Influence: Impacting Your Workplace for Christ* (Colorado Springs: NavPress, 2003); William E. Diehl, *The Monday Connection: On Being an Authentic Christian in a Weekday World* (San Francisco: HarperSanFranciso, 1991); Doug Sherman and William Hendricks, *Your Work Matters to God* (Colorado Springs: NavPress, 1987); Ed Silvoso, *Anointed for Business* (Ventura: Regal, 2002); R. Paul Stevens, *The Other Six Days: Vocation, Work, and Ministry in Biblical Perspective* (Grand Rapids: Eerdmans, 1999), *Seven Days of Faith* and *Down-to-Earth Spirituality: Encountering God in the Ordinary, Boring Stuff of Life* (Downers Grove: InterVarsity Press, 2003).

5. R. Paul Stevens, *Seven Days of Faith*, 20–21.

6. Ibid., 21–23.

7. Ibid., 23.

8. Ibid., 24.

9. R. Paul Stevens, *The Other Six Days*, 113. Also see Robert Banks, *God the Worker: Journeys into the Mind, Heart, and Imagination of God* (Sutherland, Australia: Albatross Books, 1992).

10. Stevens, *The Other Six Days*, 118.

11. R. Paul Stevens, *Down-to-Earth Spirituality*, 91.

12. See David Claerbaut, *Faith and Learning on the Edge: A Bold New Look at Religion and Higher Education* (Grand Rapids: Zondervan, 2004), and Cornelius Plantinga Jr., *Engaging God's World: A Christian Vision of Faith, Learning, and Living* (Grand Rapids: Eerdmans, 2002).

13. Doug Sherman and William Hendricks, *Your Work Matters to God*, 167.
14. Stevens, *Down-to-Earth Spirituality*, 100.
15. Ibid., 101–2.
16. Ed Silvoso, *Anointed for Business*, 33.
17. Ibid., 22.
18. Ibid., 182–92.
19. See Jack Serra, *Martketplace, Marriage, and Revival: The Spiritual Connection* (Orlando: Longwood Communications, 2001).
20. Silvoso, *Anointed for Business*, 192, 195.
21. Crane and Hamel, *Executive Influence*, 13.
22. Ibid., 93–101.
23. Ibid., 93–94. Also see Dennis W. Bakke, *Joy at Work: A Revolutionary Approach to Fun on the Job* (Seattle: PVG, 2005).
24. Randy Alcorn, *The Treasure Principle: Discovering the Secret of Joyful Giving* (Sisters: Multnomah, 2001), 17.
25. Ibid., 23, 41, 45, 49, 56, 73.
26. See Ronald J. Sider, *Just Generosity: A New Vision for Overcoming Poverty in America* (Grand Rapids: Baker, 1999), and *The Scandal of the Evangelical Conscience: Why Are Christians Living Just Like the Rest of the World?* (Grand Rapids: Baker, 2005), and Ronald J. Sider and Diane Knippers, eds., *Toward an Evangelical Public Policy: Political Strategies for the Health of the Nations* (Grand Rapids: Baker, 2005).
27. Plantinga, *Engaging God's World*, 142–43.

Chapter 14: Living for Eternity

1. John Piper, *The Purifying Power of Living by Faith in Future Grace* (Sisters: Multnomah, 1995), 20, 47.
2. Ibid., 327.
3. Ibid., 347.
4. John Eldredge, *Waking the Dead: The Glory of a Heart Fully Alive* (Nashville: Thomas Nelson, 2003), 149.
5. John Piper, *When I Don't Desire God: How to Fight for Joy* (Wheaton: Crossway, 2004), 21.
6. John Piper, *Don't Waste Your Life* (Wheaton: Crossway, 2003), 10. Also see John Piper, *God Is the Gospel: Meditations on God's Love as the Gift of Himself* (Wheaton: Crossway, 2005).
7. Randy Alcorn, *Heaven* (Wheaton: Tyndale, 2004), 155, 42.
8. Ibid., 165.
9. Ibid., 453–54.
10. Ibid., 453, 455.
11. Ibid., 457.
12. Warren, *The Purpose-Driven Life*, 263.
13. Arthur O. Roberts, *Exploring Heaven: What Great Christian Thinkers Tell Us about Our Afterlife with God* (San Francisco: HarperSanFrancisco, 2003), 168. Also see Ted Dekker, *The Slumber of Christianity: Awakening a Passion for Heaven on Earth* (Nashville: Nelson, 2005).
14. Warren Wiersbe, *On Being a Servant of God* (Grand Rapids: Baker, 1993), 146–47.
15. Anne Graham Lotz, *Heaven: My Father's House* (Nashville: W Publishing Group, 2001), 96–97.
16. See Mark R. McMinn, *Finding Our Way Home* (San Francisco: Jossey-Bass, 2005).

17. S. Y. Tan, "Medical Professionalism: Our Badge and Our Pledge," *Singapore Medical Journal* 41 (2000): 312.

18. Ibid., 315.

19. See Foster, *Celebration of Discipline*, 1.

20. Warren, *The Purpose-Driven Life*, 270.

21. Sam Sasser, *The Potter's Touch: Consecrated to Servanthood* (Shippensburg, PA: Destiny Image, 1991), 120.

22. Jack Hayford, "Spirit-Formed in Purity and Power," *Spectrum*, 6, no. 2 (Spring 2005): 5–6.

23. Eric Tiansay, "Ministry Matters/Transitions: World Relief President Resigns," *Ministries Today* (January/February, 2005): 12.

Siang-Yang Tan is professor of psychology at Fuller Theological Seminary and senior pastor of First Evangelical Church Glendale in Glendale, California. He serves on the Board and Ministry Team of RENOVARÉ, a spiritual renewal ministry founded by Richard Foster, and has written numerous books, including *Coping with Depression, Rest, Disciplines of the Holy Spirit*, and *Lay Counseling.*